SEVEN CHURCH ARC
1830 – 1930

SEVEN CHURCH ARCHITECTS
1830 – 1930

Edited by Geoff Brandwood

Ecclesiology Today · Issue 42 · June 2010

ISSN: 1460-4213
ISBN: 0 946823 24 3

Published 2010 by the Ecclesiological Society
c/o The Society of Antiquaries of London
Burlington House
Piccadilly
London
WIV 0HS

The Ecclesiological Society is a registered charity.
Charity No. 210501.

www.ecclsoc.org

Front cover: E. B. Lamb's church of St Mary, Bagby, North Yorkshire, 1862.
Rear cover: The crossing at Ewan Christian's first church, St John's, Hildenborough, Kent, 1843–4.
Both photographs by Geoff Brandwood.

Journal of the
Ecclesiological Society

Ecclesiology Today

Contents

Chairman's letter 2

Introduction
by Geoff Brandwood 3

An alternative to Ecclesiology: William Wallen (1807-53)
by Christopher Webster 9

The churches of E. B. Lamb: an exercise in
centralised planning
by Anthony Edwards 29

'The callous Mr Christian': the making and unmaking
of a professional reputation
by Martin Cherry 49

'Inventive and ingenious': designs by William White
by Gill Hunter 69

'An architect of many churches': John Pollard Seddon
by Tye R. Blackshaw 83

George Fellowes Prynne (1853-1927): a dedicated life
by Ruth Sharville 103

The ecclesiastical work of Hugh Thackeray Turner
by Robin Stannard 121

Reviews 147

The Ecclesiological Society and submissions to
Ecclesiology Today 163

Issue 42
published June 2010

Chairman's letter

This edition of *Ecclesiology Today* is devoted to seven very different church architects, whose work covers the period from late Georgian times to the first decades of the twentieth century. We are grateful to our guest editor, Dr Geoff Brandwood, for his vision and hard work in pulling together such an interesting edition.

Our next issue, due out at the end of 2010, will be devoted to the subject of church monuments, with Sally Badham as guest editor. It promises to be an intriguing set of articles.

Our new Hon. Editor, Dr Lynne Broughton, formally picks up the reins for the first edition of 2011, but has already started to shadow the process informally. As explained at the end of this volume, Lynne is keen to to continue receiving offers of articles on a wide range of topics connected to churches and their furnishings, so do contact her if you have something in mind.

Finally, as already explained to members in more detail in a separate communication, the monograph dedicated to pews and church seating will now be published as a separate book, and not as an edition of *Ecclesiology Today*. Members will receive it free of charge.

Trevor Cooper
Chairman of Council

Introduction

THIS VOLUME brings together essays on seven architects on whom very little or, in some cases, nothing has been published before. They and their work are very diverse but all of them, with the exception of Thackeray Turner, made Anglican church building and restoration the main focus of their careers. Their work, collectively, spans very nearly a century, from the closing years of the Georgian era to shortly after the First World War, and reflects a wide variety of churchmanship on the part of the architects themselves, and the patrons, clergy and congregations who commissioned them. Victorian and Edwardian churches are anything but homogeneous as this volume clearly shows.

For many architects in the period under scrutiny, church work was something very special. Not surprisingly, those who concentrated on this field were usually devout churchmen themselves. They viewed their commissions as an important way of serving the Christian Church, by providing proper settings for divine worship and from which the Church's wider mission could be spread. Furthermore, churches, apart from the very humblest, gave opportunities for architectural expression which were simply not possible in run-of-the-mill projects that made up (and, of course, still make up) the bulk of building activity. Church-building was prestigious and secured attention. A new church would attract widespread local interest; the foundation stone and consecration ceremonies would be attended by large numbers of people and be reported in the local press; and also there was even a reasonable chance of getting a notice (or, indeed, an illustration) into one or other of the architectural journals.

As is well known, the years around 1840 saw a revolution in the way churches were designed and fitted up. Change had been a long time in gestation with many strands coalescing and many individuals playing a part. In numerous shorthand summaries of what took place, Pugin and his polemical writings, which started to appear in 1836, and the Cambridge Camden Society, founded in 1839, are cited as the prime movers behind the physical changes that took place. They made sure, as Christopher Webster points out in his essay, that they wrote themselves into history accordingly. The Cambridge society and its less strident counterpart in Oxford were, in fact, incredibly successful in promoting the 'science' of ecclesiology and the 'correct' way of

Geoff Brandwood has written widely on church architecture of the Victorian period including a monograph on Temple Moore, and is a former chairman of the Victorian Society. He is currently completing a study of the great north-western practice of Paley and Austin.

building and fitting up a church. Such success has, of course, to be seen in the context of two other major developments. One of these was an intense interest in all things medieval, which was an integral part of north European Romanticism: the other was the not unrelated Oxford Movement/Tractarianism which, while not having any architectural agenda itself, often underpinned the attitudes of those who did.

By the end of the 1840s the new ways had triumphed, the most visible of which was the hegemony of Gothic. It had become the only acceptable style for Anglicans of all leanings as few now saw it as tainted with the odour of Popery. For Roman Catholics too it was becoming the style of choice and provided a connection to a Catholic past that had been ruptured at the Reformation. Even some Nonconformists, normally very wary of Popish associations, were beginning to take it up, starting with the Congregationalists. Although the particular forms of Gothic style that had flourished at the end of the thirteenth-century and in early fourteenth century were adopted by those occupying the ecclesiological and architectural high-ground, their preferences were not universally adopted, as this volume will show. Also, as the second half of the nineteenth century progressed, the idea of developing Gothic bore fruit, often with exotic results. But whatever the details of the style that was used, it was still the architecture of the Middle Ages which underpinned most church-building until the interwar period, and sometimes beyond, as Coventry Cathedral shows.

Hand in hand with the establishment of a new orthodoxy about style went changed desiderata for how churches were to be arranged. What Puginian-Ecclesiological teaching established in the 1840s became the norm for Anglican and Roman Catholic churches for over a century and which only began to be unpicked by reordering movements in both Churches in the latter part of the twentieth century. By 1850 the accoutrements of the Georgian Anglican church – such as short or virtually non-existent chancels, box-pews, galleries, plaster ceilings, and pulpits placed on the centre-line of the nave in front of the chancel arch – had given way to very different arrangements which formed the material expression of changing attitudes towards the conduct of worship and the reverence in the Church and its buildings were (or were meant to be) held.

The essays in this volume examine a number of very diverse church architects from the late Georgian period onwards (in, it has to be said, an almost exclusively Anglican context). They show that the generalisations above are no more than that and they illustrate some of the many shifts and subtle nuances in church architecture and fittings in the extraordinarily complex century under review.

The first essay deals with a Yorkshire architect who will be unfamiliar to most readers, William Wallen (1807–53). He is, nonetheless, an interesting character, brought out of the shadows by Christopher Webster who has made a special study of church-building in late Georgian/early Victorian England. Like others of his generation, Wallen took an early scholarly interest in medieval antiquities and he made useful contributions to the growing stock of publications which helped underpin knowledge about them. Leaving London behind, he set up practice in the West Riding and built a number of churches from 1838. Although Wallen had an excellent knowledge of medieval architecture, it is most interesting that his designs were deliberately anti-Camdenian and he included, for example, galleries in all his churches. It is therefore salutary to realise that there were architects who, as Christopher Webster's paper entitles it, offered an alternative to Ecclesiology. His study therefore usefully complements that of Wallen's un-Ecclesiological contemporary, George Wightwick (1802–76), published by Rosamund Reid in 2000.[1]

E. B. Lamb (1805–69) was of the same generation of Wallen and Wightwick and he too did not subscribe to Ecclesiological orthodoxy. Anthony Edwards is an architect himself who has recently completed his Ph.D on Lamb. Here he looks at Lamb's work through professional eyes and uses computer technology to understand the principles behind his planning. Many of Lamb's highly individual churches are quite well-known but, as is shown here, they are not the product simply of eccentric architectural caprice. The stylistic dress was Gothic sure enough, but the planning was new and intended specifically to address mid-nineteenth-century Anglican needs. That he could find clients, notably his regular patrons, Lord and Lady Frankland Russell, shows that there were those who were not always looking for the straightforward Ecclesiological solution.

The third essay deals with an (perhaps *the*) establishment church architect *par excellence*, Ewan Christian (1814–95), who was just a few years younger than Wallen and Lamb. He was prodigiously productive, especially as the architect to the Ecclesiastical Commissioners for most of his working life, and was admired for his efficiency, bringing jobs in on time and within budget. While such virtues are admired by most clients, architectural history has not been kindly in its judgement of Christian, and it is the question of his reputation, both in his lifetime and subsequently, that is explored by Martin Cherry. No real claims can be made that Christian was in the top flight of Victorian church architects but does his best work not warrant greater appreciation than it has? Was it all a High Church conspiracy (after all, that was the winning side by the start of the twentieth century when it comes to ecclesiastical architecture)?

William White (1825–1900) is an excellent representative of the new generation of church-builders who started out in the changing world of the 1840s. He joined the Ecclesiological Society in 1848 just after setting up in practice, and was of High Church persuasion although he was unsympathetic to the more extreme practices that, in due course, developed into ritualism. By the early years of his career, the Ecclesiological movement, having successfully campaigned for the faithful reuse of English medieval precedents, was starting progress along new paths, exemplified most famously by Butterfield and his client. Beresford Hope's, project to build All Saints, Margaret Street in the heart of central London. Innovation was possible and, indeed, sought after as an expression of the developing Church. As with the liturgical results of ritualism, church architecture could take some extravagant forms. Although not guilty of wilder excesses of 'acrobatic Gothic' (as the *Building News* dubbed it in 1864),[2] White did create highly imaginative, colourful architecture. His work has been the subject of research by Gill Hunter which gained her a Ph.D in 2007 and is now being published in book form, thus giving this interesting architect the exposure he rightly deserves.[3] In the present volume she explores the enthusiasm for new techniques and ideas on the part of the 'inventive and ingenious' Mr White.

The churches of John Pollard Seddon (1827–1906) are examined by Tye Blackshaw who completed a Ph.D on the architect in 2001. Seddon was a very close contemporary of White. but, whereas White produced some striking buildings from the very start of his career, Seddon's early work was fairly minor, much of it Welsh church restorations in partnership with John Prichard (1817–86). By the late 1850s, however, Seddon, a Broad Churchman, a friend of several key Pre-Raphaelites, and an active member of the Ecclesiological Society (from 1857), was producing some interesting churches. Like White, he loved architectural colour and sought imaginative and innovative architectural effects. He had a particular love of the robust early medieval architecture of Normandy and this found its way into a number of his buildings. This was typical of the way continental forms crept into English church architecture in the High Victorian period, just as continental liturgical practices would be adopted by some of the more advanced ritualists of the time. Seddon resolutely resisted the changing character of church architecture from the 1870s and remained true to his High Victorian architectural roots.

The best late Victorian and Edwardian churches are indeed very different from those of the mid-Victorian years. They are less strident and muscular, and rely for their effect on proportion and line, as well as often embracing later medieval forms that had been sidelined in the 1840s. They have far less ornament, and decorative richness resides not in the architecture but individual fixtures and fittings George Fellowes Prynne (1853–1927) is one of the best representatives of this changed aesthetic and the Anglican Church it served. He began his career some thirty years after White and Seddon and was a devout Anglo-Catholic who saw his art as a means of expressing his faith, as Ruth Sharville, who has been cataloguing his life and works, explains. By the end of the nineteenth century the requirement for new churches in the countryside had largely been satisfied and most of Fellowes Prynne's work is for new town churches or for furnishings and fittings. Devastated by losses from within his own family in the Great War, he continued to practice after 1918 although, for a number of years, as for all church architects, demands for his services were largely confined to memorialising the fallen.

The last architect is Hugh Thackeray Turner (1853–1937), born in the same year as Fellowes Prynne, but with a very different career profile and personal ethos. Unlike all the other figures in this volume, each of whom can be seen as primarily church architects, Thackeray Turner is best known for his work as Secretary of the Society for the Preservation of Ancient Buildings, which from its foundation in 1877, did so much to influence opinion against the kind of intrusive church restoration that had been taking place during the past thirty years. Robin Stannard, a historic building surveyor, has, for a number of years, been studying Thackeray Turner's work, and here he examines the ecclesiastical side of his career. He was one of those who trained under Gilbert Scott but who reacted against the values of their master. Indeed, he turned his back on the whole idea of the Gothic Revival and was responsible for two remarkable London churches which broke with the traditions of mainstream design and which are considered in detail here.

It is hoped that this collection of essays will help increase the profile of the architects portrayed and also add something to the wider understanding of a hundred-year period which had a greater impact on our churches than any comparable length of time since the Middle Ages.

Acknowledgements

I am grateful to Martin Cherry and Trevor Cooper for reading a draft of this introduction and making a number of helpful suggestions.

NOTES

1 'George Wightwick: a Thorn in the Side of the Ecclesiologists' in Christopher Webster and John Elliott (eds.), *'A Church as it should be': The Cambridge Camden Society and its Influence* (Stamford, 2000).239–56. Another interesting case is Edmund Sharpe of Lancaster who, was at once an expert on medieval architecture, like Wallen, (he was awarded the RIBA Royal Gold Medal in 1875 for his writings), and a staunch Low Churchman who belonged to the Protestant Association.

2 11, 1864, 780.

3 *William White, Pioneer Victorian Architect* (Reading, 2010).

An alternative to Ecclesiology: William Wallen (1807–1853)

Christopher Webster

BY THE MID-1840s, once Ecclesiology had become firmly established, phrases such as the following became commonplace among the church-building fraternity:

> the design shows … a want of mature knowledge … ;[1]
> [the architect] has shown that his signal failure is owing to nothing but his own insufficient acquaintance with the art he professes;[2]
> this church is so unpleasing in its treatment, is so sham in its proposed groining, and so much below the average of the ecclesiastical knowledge and taste of the present day.[3]

Christopher Webster is an architectural historian who specialises in the first half of the nineteenth century. He is particularly interested in the stylistic shift from the Classical tradition to the Gothic Revival, especially the role played in this by the Cambridge Camden Society and the regional architectural societies. His R.D. Chantrell (1793–1872) and the Architecture of a Lost Generation was published earlier this year.

To be acclaimed as a successful architect in Ecclesiological circles was rather like belonging to an exclusive club whose members looked down with a mixture of pity and disdain on those who aspired to join, but lacked the necessary credentials. William Wallen, who began his career as a church architect in 1838, on the very eve of the formation of the Cambridge Camden Society, produced a series of churches that are easily overlooked today and never came near the dizzy heights of real acclamation in his own lifetime. Yet whatever indifference might have greeted his designs, Wallen could never be accused of 'a want of mature knowledge'. Indeed, it would be hard to imagine *any* architect setting out to establish a church practice around 1840, in those heady days of the newly discovered and potent mixture of Gothic architecture and Anglicanism's Catholic roots, who could boast a better preparation.

Wallen in London

Wallen was born in 1807,[4] the son of the architect John Wallen (1785–1865), and died young, still only in his forties.[5] The family lived in a series of houses in, or adjacent to Spital Square, Spitalfields in London, from where John ran his practice. His work listed by Colvin[6] – some minor country house alterations, repairs to buildings owned by charities and several warehouses – might suggest he ran an entirely unremarkable practice, and produced little of architectural note. However, Wallen senior's practice *is* remarkable in two respects. Firstly, he had been a pupil of Daniel Alexander (1768–1846), who excelled at the design of large industrial buildings, warehouses, prisons and dockyards, and had a number of very important surveyorships in the City. Alexander's interest in this somewhat specialised area of architectural practice

Fig. 1: Holmbridge, near Huddersfield, St David, 1838–40. The dates here are crucial: the nave and tower are not untypical of 1838, but the overall design could be dismissed as deeply conservative by the time of the consecration.

seems to have informed John Wallen's own career. John might have produced few landmark buildings, but this sector of practice, often involving huge budgets, provided an essential component in Britain's industrial supremacy. Secondly, John had several pupils who went on to enjoy notable careers, and it seems that the training he offered was of an exceptional standard. Pupils included Horace Jones (1819–1887) who had an outstanding career as Architect to the City of London, and was subsequently knighted for his achievements.[7] Also in Wallen's office was Edward I'Anson (1812–88) whose glittering years of practice were crowned by the presidency of the RIBA in 1886–7.[8] I'Anson initially trained in the office of his architect father – also called Edward (1775–1853) – and it is surely significant that it was deemed beneficial for the son subsequently to spend some time with Wallen to complete his education. Wallen was described in an 1890 reference as 'principal quantity surveyor [in the 1830s] in the City',[9] and it seems reasonable to conclude that he continued that branch of practice begun by Alexander that concentrated on the essential and lucrative, if unglamorous, area of large-scale industrial building, and building maintenance.

William Wallen thus enjoyed an exceptionally thorough architectural education in his father's office. His uncle – also William (d. 1857) – his father's older brother, was a surveyor who is credited with at least two architectural commissions.[10] Perhaps young William had some experience in his office too. The formal part of his pupillage is likely to have been completed around 1828, by which time he would have been 21. There is then a ten-year gap before he began independent practice in Huddersfield.

How did he pass the decade? On the domestic front, he married in 1830 and a son – another William – arrived in 1831. Through the early and mid-1830s, William, his wife Frances (born 1804) and his son continued to live with his parents at 11 Spital Square in Spitalfields.[11] It was a substantial brick house of three storeys plus cellars and attics, built around 1700. The family's neighbours included a number of the area's major silk manufacturers. Certainly William was working in his father's practice by 1831, when the firm was known as Wallen, Son and Beatson,[12] but what we know of William's subsequent career would suggest he might have had little sympathy with the sort of work passing through the office. His interests seem to have leant much more towards what might be termed the more conventional areas of architecture: the production of traditional building types in a variety of historical styles. It is known, too, that William was busy with a series of disparate activities in the 1830s – which will be addressed shortly – that surely would have restricted the time he could devote to his father's firm. Perhaps a combination of his external interests and his father's not inconsiderable fee income persuaded John to allow his son some freedom to pursue antiquarian and other interests, and this was precisely the path followed two decades earlier by two of William's best friends of the period, to whom we must now turn.

Wallen's activities in his twenties are intimately linked with those of Edward Cresy (1792–1858)[13] and George Ledwell Taylor (1888–1873).[14] Both worked as architects and civil engineers, and both were keen archaeologists. Both also came from comfortable middle-class families and seem to have had the means to pursue their antiquarian interests through their twenties before settling into careers. Perhaps it was accounts of their travels and continental adventures that prompted Wallen to persuade his own family to support him in his third decade and release him from the

Fig. 2: Holmbridge, St David, 1838–40. East end, from a nineteenth-century photograph. A substantial chancel was subsequently added. The total absence of a chancel in a scheme of 1838 is remarkable. However, this seems to derive from Wallen's Low Church sympathies, rather than his ignorance of current trends.

Fig. 3: Farsley, Leeds, St John the Evangelist, 1842–3. Wallen's executed chancel was significantly longer than the one shown here and the upper section of the tower was also modified before construction. Despite the decent size of the chancel, this is still very much a pre-Camdenian design. (WYAS Leeds, BDP 26/31)

demands of full-time work in an office on the understanding he would apply himself to a respectable career later. Having said that, the first notice of Wallen's activities beyond his father's firm concerned the debates that surrounded the organisation of the architectural profession, suggesting he was not that far removed from the rigours of practice. Prior to the establishment of the Institute of British Architects in 1834 – later the RIBA – a number of alternative societies and professional groupings were being promoted, especially in the early 1830s. Cresy and Taylor – by now well established as architects and surveyors – occupied prominent positions in the discussions that led to the various factions uniting to form the IBA, indeed Cresy was the chairman of a group interested in architectural topography and was on the joint committee that thrashed out the prospectus for the Institute. Earlier, he and Taylor had been members of the Architects' and Antiquaries' Club, probably also members of the Architectural Society,[15] and both were founder members of the IBA, although Cresy did not long continue his membership.[16] While Wallen is not recorded as a key figure in these discussions, Cresy, writing later lamenting the state of British architecture added: 'The Institute of British Architects ought to have done something to remove the obloquy clouding the noble profession, and in my early days I laid the foundations with my friend Wallen for a society of men who would act in concert.'[17] That Cresy singles out Wallen from a number of young architects who are known to have agitated for better architectural education and professional status is surely significant. And there were other matters that brought Wallen into contact with Cresy and Taylor, and through them to a number of very prominent architects and antiquaries.

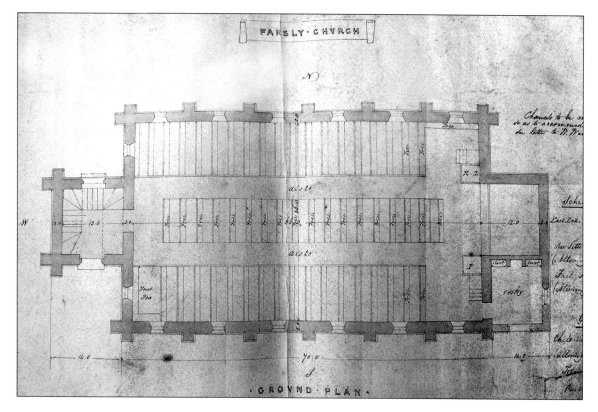

Fig. 4: Farsley, St John the Evangelist, 1842–3, plan. (WYAS, Leeds, BDP 26/31)

Antiquarian interests

An organisation that drew together this trio's interest in antiquarianism and topography was the little-known Topographical Society, founded around 1836, perhaps the result of Cresy's dissatisfaction with the early direction taken by the IBA. The TS's initial prospectus suggests it was intended to publish a twice-yearly journal comprising a 'miscellany of genealogical and topographical material such as hitherto unpublished wills, cartularies etc'.[18] Wallen was its secretary, and his home in Spital Square was the society's address for correspondence. Wallen's antiquarian interests had already been brought to the public's attention as between 1828 and 1833 he exhibited a total of eight items at Royal Academy exhibitions, mainly depictions of medieval buildings, interestingly describing himself in the catalogues as 'painter' rather than 'architect'.

Wallen did not join the IBA, but seems to have continued as a member of the Architectural Society which remained independent after the formation of the IBA and was eventually wound up only in 1842.[19] Wallen was certainly a member of the AS in 1836 when he presented its library with two books,[20] although, interestingly, at the same time he also presented the IBA library with a copy of his *Little Maplestead*, published that year.

Wallen's *The History and Antiquities of the Round Church at Little Maplestead, Essex* is of interest here for a number of reasons. The church was of considerable antiquarian importance as one of only a handful of circular churches, all associated with the Knights Hospitaller, based on the model of the church of the Holy Sepulchre at Jerusalem. Little Maplestead is a late example, probably of around 1335, replacing a twelfth-century original.[21] Despite Wallen's choice of title which confidently announces an antiquarian agenda, the contents must have disappointed many: it is, essentially, a history not of the church, but of the Crusades and of the knights. Only at page 125 – of 159 – do we reach 'The Manor of Maplestead' and the church itself comes in the last chapter, from page 145. Even then there is a long account of the 'structures erected by the early Christians, in order to point out the circumstances that seem to have induced them to give the preference to a circular form',[22] which relies heavily on Sir George Wheler's published work. In Wallen's defence, what a twenty-first-century reader would consider to be legitimate architectural history was rare in the early nineteenth century and most church histories were little more than lists of vicars, endowments and charities. We should not be too hard on Wallen.[23] His final chapter is, eventually, a thorough and commendably diligent piece of research, entirely compatible with modern standards. It reveals its author to be familiar with the writings of Rickman, and the antiquaries Stukeley, Fosbroke, Gough and Dallaway. Additionally, he had undertaken a 'careful investigation, made by kind permission of the present incumbent',[24] which involved excavations both inside and outside the church in an attempt to ascertain its original form. In order to date parts of the building, Wallen had compared them to similar features in other Essex churches where there was documentary confirmation of their period of erection.[25] The text is complemented by sixteen small wood engravings and eight plates – all by Wallen – including a plan, a section, two details and several perspective views. The 'history' of the church is no more than nine pages, but it is a commendable piece of work from a writer who had adopted the very highest standards of contemporary scholarship and it received a positive review in the *Architectural Magazine*.[26]

The book repays attention in a number of other contexts and the list of subscribers is fascinating. Firstly, it reveals twelve of them were from Huddersfield and its immediate surroundings. That Wallen had these contacts is surely a convincing explanation for his hitherto unlikely arrival in the town two years after publication. Secondly, the list reveals much about the young Wallen's standing in the national architectural scene. The book attracted 510 subscribers which, for the first work by a man still

Fig. 5: Farsley, St John the Evangelist, 1842–3. This recent photograph eloquently conveys the extent to which Wallen's interiors were at variance with those promoted by the Ecclesiologists. (Mark Saville)

in his late twenties[27] was remarkable enough, but analysis of them is also illuminating.

Books like this on individual churches were not uncommon in this period. The market was essentially antiquarian rather than architectural and subscribers were predominantly made up of the aristocracy and gentry, clergy, schoolmasters and members of antiquarian societies; Wallen's book is quite exceptional for the quantity and quality of its architectural subscribers. The list contains 106 architects – more than 20 per cent of the total – and includes Soane and Nash at the very top of the profession, Cockerell, Bonomi, Cottingham, Salvin and Burn just a little below them, and amongst those who would later become the young Turks of the Gothic Revival were Pugin, Ferrey and Carpenter; it included no less than four of 'His Majesty's Commissioners appointed to inspect the designs for the new Houses of Parliament' and 'W.B. Clark Esq., President of the Architectural Society, London'. It was impressive support. By way of context, Marmaduke Prickett's *An Historical and Architectural Description of the Priory Church of Bridlington*, published just five years earlier, had a slightly longer list of subscribers but it included just one architect.

How much of Wallen's time is it likely to have consumed? It is impossible to say, but at a time when this sort of study was in its infancy and published material on the subject, on which Wallen could have drawn, was limited, it is hard to see how it could have been undertaken while its author had a full-time job. Simply completing the paperwork to secure the 510 subscriptions must have been a Herculean task in itself.

By the time it was published, Wallen was busy with his next publishing project, *Illustrations of Stone Church, Kent*. It was first announced in 1836,[28] in a letter that appeared in the *Gentleman's*

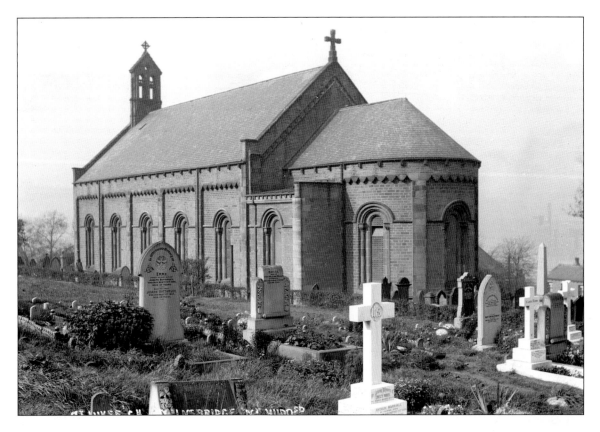

Fig. 6: Milnsbridge, near Huddersfield, St Luke, 1843–5. This was Wallen's first Norman composition, and his first design with a bellcote instead of a tower. (Kirklees Image Archive)

Magazine.[29] The project was promoted by the Topographical Society and the letter was signed by Wallen as the society's secretary. It stated that Wallen himself was preparing a history of this important thirteenth-century church and other members of the society would supply the illustrations. It was to be the society's first publication and the notice suggested it would be an impressive one. Probably as a result of his departure for Huddersfild in 1838, Wallen seems to have taken no further part in the project and the book, which was eventually published in 1840, records Cresy as its author although five woodcut illustrations by Wallen are included.[30]

While Wallen was in the process of completing *Little Maplestead* and extending the subscription list, he became a fellow of the Society of Antiquaries, the committee meeting of 18 June 1835 confirming the election.[31] The testimonial that accompanied his application was signed by Cresy and Taylor, as well as J. B. Nichols[32] and P. F. Robinson.[33] The minute book describes Wallen as 'a Gentleman very conversant with the History and Antiquities of this Kingdom'; although it was a more or less standard one in use by applicants at the time, it was nevertheless a commendable achievement for a twenty-eight year old.

Fig. 7: Milnsbridge, St Luke, 1843–5. This late nineteenth-century photograph is fascinating. While the painted decoration of the apse is post-Wallen, the decoration of the chancel arch and the arcading behind the altar reveal Wallen's progressive attitude to the Norman style. Even the gallery fronts are appropriately Norman. (Kirklees Image Archive)

Wallen in Yorkshire

In 1838, Wallen appeared in Huddersfield. On one level, this seems to have been a most unlikely career development, but, as has been mentioned in connection with *Littler Maplestead*, he must already have had contacts in the town.[34] No doubt they had informed him that despite the huge amount of development taking place there, it had no resident architect. The first mention of him in Huddersfield comes in connection with the new church at Holmbridge with which Wallen was involved from March 1838,[35] perhaps his first independent job anywhere.[36] The *Leeds Intelligencer* of 27 October 1838 announced Wallen as the victor in the Huddersfield Collegiate School competition, and the same edition carried an advertisement stating Wallen had moved from his London address – listed as Great Marlborough Street – to Burton Road, Huddersfield.[37] Before we turn our attention to his designs for churches, there are two additional subjects that can usefully be explored, both of which help amplify our understanding of Wallen's interests: his involvement with the Yorkshire Architectural Society and the publication of his *Two Essays*.

Fig. 8: Oakworth, near Keighley, Christ Church, 1844–6. The tower has lost its pinnacles, and the lower tower window and the upper vesica piscis *shaped windows in the nave were, originally, glazed.*

Wallen was a founder and, initially, very active member of the Yorkshire Architectural Society, one of a number of provincial groups established in the 1840s in the wake of the pioneering work of the Cambridge Camden Society and Oxford Architectural Society. These societies were sometimes referred to as 'diocesan architectural societies' and while the term 'architectural' implied broad interests, their focus was much narrower. The Yorkshire group's objective was 'to promote the study of Ecclesiastical Architecture, Antiquities and Design, the restoration of mutilated architectural remains and of Churches or parts of Churches which may have been desecrated, within the County of York; and to improve, so far as may be within its province, the character of Ecclesiastical Edifices to be erected in future.'[38] Like the others, the Yorkshire group was dominated by the clergy, but at its first formal meeting after formation, it was agreed, 'Those architects who really understand the principles of Gothic architecture and of ecclesiastical design, and only want

Fig. 9: Oakworth, Christ Church, 1844–6. The east end is plain and dignified, although the shallow chancel and the low pitch of the roofs remain rooted in pre-Ecclesiological thinking.

room, and liberty, and a just appreciation of their talents to distinguish themselves will, we are persuaded, find in the Yorkshire Architectural Society a very effective ally.' Indeed, Wallen, as the first architect member, was present to hear these words from the chairman, and over the next few years he would be joined by most of the leading Yorkshire architects who specialised in church work – R. D. Chantrell arrived soon after Wallen – along with others from further away like L. N. Cottingham. It was at this first meeting, on 29 September 1842, that Wallen was elected to the committee.

During its early years, he appears to have been a diligent supporter and a regular attendee of committee meetings, despite these initially being held at a variety of locations round this very large county. He was at the first general meeting in York in October 1842, and at the committee meeting a month later when he presented the society with 'an illuminated copy' of his book on Little Maplestead church, possibly the first item acquired for the library. He was at the meeting in December in Howden when he and Chantrell were invited to join a small sub-committee to advise on the restoration of the minster there. At the next meeting in Wakefield, in February 1843, Wallen proposed his old friend Cresy for membership and he, along with Chantrell again, formed part of the sub-committee to oversee work at the Chantry Chapel in Wakefield – the Society's first restoration project – a

Fig. 10: Whitehaven, Cumbria (Cumberland), Christ Church, 1845–7. How Wallen came to win this commission has not been discovered. The use of Norman and the inclusion of a bellcote link the design to Milnsbridge, but the plan – especially the symmetrical south front with centrally placed entrance and absence of even an alcove for the altar – is highly unusual. The east elevation, with a range of high level windows, is also idiosyncratic. (Lambeth Palace Library)

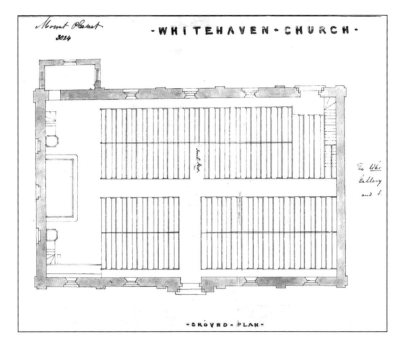

commission awarded to Scott and Moffatt. At the second annual meeting held in York in October 1843, Wallen read his paper on 'The Geometrical Principles of Gothic Architecture', a subject to which we will return later, and after the committee meeting in Halifax in November he repeated it.[39] He – and Chantrell – were re-elected to the committee at the October 1844 meeting, but neither attended any meetings during the year and were not re-elected to the committee at the annual meeting of October 1845. Were they just too busy elsewhere to continue? Possibly, but having initially been such active members, one is left wondering if there had been some fall-out.[40] On the other hand, Wallen was still an ordinary member in 1850, and probably remained one until his death.[41]

Wallen's *Two Essays Elucidating the Geometrical Principles of Gothic Architecture*, the basis for the YAS lectures mentioned above, were initially delivered to the Geological and Polytechnic Society of the West Riding of Yorkshire late in 1841 and published in Leeds in 1842. They were, no doubt, a significant means of bringing him into the orbit of the society's clerical founders. Identifying the principles which had informed the architects of the great medieval cathedrals, abbeys and churches was a subject that exercised many a Gothic scholar through the nineteenth century.[42] Once again, Cresy emerges as a possible starting point for Wallen's own treatise, and almost exactly concurrently, Wallen's architect friend from the YAS, Chantrell, was investigating the subject independently, and reaching different conclusions. It is impossible to know which of these three led the investigations and which followed, although there must have been some exchanging of ideas. Cresy's detailed conclusions did not appear until 1847, in his *Encyclopaedia of Civil Engineering* – although he touches on the subject in publications from the 1820s – and they reappeared verbatim in Wyatt Papwoth's revised editions of Joseph Gwilt's *Encyclopaedia of Architecture* from 1867.

Wallen recognised a clear need for identifiable principles. 'We have "Glossaries of Gothic Architecture" and Archaeological Dictionaries defining the *names* of the details, [yet] we look in vain for works elucidating the actual *principles* of the pointed style.' [43] Summarising his attempt to satisfy this need is neither easy in the space available here, nor does it do justice to his undoubtedly diligent research. Wallen believed that the medieval architects used simple mathematical ratios in setting out the plans and elevations of their buildings, often the module was half the width of the nave. Making use of the measurements to be found in Britton's *Cathedral Antiquities*, he showed that, for instance, the internal width of York Minster is 106 feet, thus the module is 53. The nave is four modules long and the crossing one module. He also explores the possibilities of the *vesica piscis* – a theory given much support by Papworth – which was the basis of Chantrell's system. The idea that any such system of design was used consistently throughout Europe and over several centuries, has enjoyed little support among more recent commentators, but perhaps its real importance in the context of this paper is that Wallen's publication linked him with some of the country's major archaeologist/architects like C. R. Cockerell and must have significantly enhanced his reputation among the Yorkshire church-building fraternity. It also contains the only evidence to come to light of Wallen's attitudes to the design of modern churches.

Wallen makes it clear he has 'devoted much attention to the subject' of medieval proportions and exhorts other architects to do likewise: they must have 'a practical acquaintance with [Gothic's] real principles ... personal investigation of our ancient edifices is absolutely necessary ... we must first analyse the details, then study the whole composition, and until this be done, our minds cannot be imbued with the feelings of the master-spirits of former ages.' [44]

Wallen's churches

Finally then, we can address the issue of his church designs. In the course of his first decade in Huddersfield, he was responsible for six new churches: Holmbridge, near Huddersfield, 1838–40,

Fig. 11: Shepley, near Huddersfield, St Paul, 1845–8. Wallen's final church was without even a modest chancel. The style is essentially Early English, although the east window reveals Wallen's sole diversion to Decorated. (WYAS, Wakefield, WDP60, add box 7)

St David (Figs. 1 & 2);[45] Farsley, Leeds, St John the Evangelist, 1842–3 (Figs. 3–5);[46] Milnsbridge, Huddersfield, St Luke, 1843–5 (Figs. 6 & 7);[47] Oakworth, near Keighley, Christ Church, 1844–6 (Figs. 8 & 9);[48] Whitehaven, Cumbria (Cumberland), St Nicholas, 1845–7 (Fig. 10);[49] Shepley, Huddersfield, St Paul, 1845–8 (Figs. 11 & 12).[50]

It would be hard to imagine an architect setting out on a church-building career who could boast better qualifications for the task or who had more impressive external interests in the early years of that career, yet examination of his designs might cause some surprise; these designs have little in common with the concurrent work of the Camdenian protégés, or of those established architects desperate to gain the approbation of the society by adopting its preferred models.

Many historians of the early Victorian period have become somewhat blinkered by the pervasive propaganda of the Cambridge Camden Society to the extent that what was deemed a failure in its eyes continues to be marginalized. But perhaps not all architects were committed to emulating the paradigms of R. C. Carpenter, G. G. Scott and, nearer to Huddersfield, Wallen's friend Chantrell in Leeds. If we can accept that Wallen had little interest in reproducing fourteenth-century Decorated idioms with steeply-pitched roofs, long chancels and (supposedly) medieval seating arrangements, we are liberated from the highly subjective confines of Camdenian 'success'. Wallen certainly had an academic interest in the architecture of the Middle Ages,[51] but, it seems, his approach to the design of modern churches was much more inventive and pragmatic, especially when budgets were small as was invariably the case with his commissions. A particularly revealing passage from his *Essays* is this: he condemns those who believe 'every pointed building must be a cathedral or nothing;

nor shall we attempt to *copy* some vast church within a twentieth part of the space, and with a hundredth part of the money.'[52] Evidence that Wallen took a consciously anti-Camdenian stance – or, indeed, any stance – is frustratingly elusive, although there are one or two hints in that direction. His *Essays* include his opinion that in all but the largest churches, 'the width does not justify the inclusion of aisles':[53] they spoil the proportions and mask the pulpit from parts of the congregation. In the heady days of the Camdenian revolution, this was a refreshingly independent and rational idea. And the inclusion of west galleries in all his churches in order to produce a satisfactory level of accommodation was equally reactionary. Secondly, John Weale, Wallen's publisher for *Little Maplestead*, was well-known for his opposition to the Camden Society, especially in his *Quarterly Papers in Architecture*, a journal whose brief life-span coincides neatly with much of Wallen's church work. Thirdly, Burfield includes material suggesting that Cresy was by no means committed to Camdenian principles and was positively against at least some of its prescriptions.[54] Cresy and Wallen might well have shared views on this as they did on so many other things.

Wallen has left few comments about style, although his *Essays* include his belief that 'late-Gothic' was 'gorgeous'.[55] However, rather than adopt this, or Decorated – the Camdenian favourite – his churches are all either Norman or Early English, a stylistic selection perhaps informed by the limited budgets. Yet even with modest funds, these churches are not dull or bare. Indeed, the combination of a Norman chancel arch with over-sized decoration, supported by debased Corinthian half-columns at Milnsbridge (Fig. 7) or the incorporation of the *vesica piscis* as a decorative motif at Holmbridge (Fig. 2) and Oakworth (Fig. 8), suggest Wallen had little interest in archaeological fidelity but was, perhaps, a pioneer in the drive to *develop* Gothic as a modern idiom, a concept subsequently promoted eloquently by Beresford Hope and his circle.[56]

How well were Wallen's churches received? The simple answer seems to be enthusiastically. At their openings, Holmbridge was described as 'pretty and commodious'[57] and Milnsbridge as 'elegant'.[58] None of Wallen's church work reached the attention of *The Ecclesiologist*, or any other section of the national press. However, Farsley was covered in R. V. Taylor's *Churches of Leeds*, 1875. The Revd Taylor was a well-informed commentator and the book's long introduction reveals his thinking to have been close to that of the early Ecclesiologists, for instance when it came to pronouncements about chancels, steps to the altar and uniform

seating, and when he is celebrating the 'present day's … philanthropy' in the building and beautifying of churches.[59] However, when he reaches the churches in Leeds, he is at least as keen to extol the increases in church provision as he is to rehearse standard criticisms of churches which clearly fell outside the confines of Ecclesiological principles. Indeed, writing about Farsley's church, thirty years after its consecration and during which time tastes had 'matured', he was still remarkably positive: 'we have scarcely, if ever, seen so neat a religious structure erected for so small a sum as this, and the design of the building, and the care with which every part is finished, do great credit to the professional skill and taste of W. Wallen Esq.'[60]

Conclusions

What conclusions can be drawn about Wallen's churches? It would be easy to dismiss them as old-fashioned for their date, mock the continued inclusion of, for instance, west galleries and modest chancels, and conclude that their designer was incapable of adjusting to the new Camdenian imperatives. Since we know Wallen was exceptionally well versed in medieval Gothic, we must find alternative explanations. With some justification, we might conclude Wallen was part of an informal group of architects – perhaps quite a large constituency, now almost entirely overlooked – which saw Anglicanism as rather 'lower' than the Camden Society's vision of it. They produced churches that, in many ways, differed little from those of the pre-Camdenian era, but not because they had a 'want of knowledge', but because they believed them to answer the demands of modern *Protestant* congregations.[61]

George Wightwick in Devon and Edmund Sharpe in Lancaster are among the few in this group to have hitherto received any serious interest. Patronage is central to this discussion; early-nineteenth-century Huddersfield was noted as a stronghold of Evangelicalism and several of Wallen's churches can, with certainty, be linked to this branch of Anglicanism.[62] Wallen gave his congregations precisely the internal arrangements they required. And it should also not be overlooked that to build as the Camden Society wanted to build was usually expensive, and Wallen's clients were, in every instance, pitifully impecunious. The 1845 edition of the *Leeds Intelligencer* that reported the opening of Milnsbridge church also noted the completion of J. M. Derrick's St Saviour's, Leeds, an early model of the new Camdenian thinking. The latter had cost around £17,000 and even then, was without its intended tower; it held just 600 worshippers.[63] Milnsbridge had required a mere £2,500, including 'all its fittings and hot water heating system' and provided places for 945.

Perhaps the story of mid nineteenth-century church-building is a classic example of the axiom 'it is the victor that writes the history of the war'. In this case it was the Ecclesiologists that triumphed, and rarely can any winning side have been more adept at marginalizing the views of the defeated opposition. Yet we should not forget that opposition to Ecclesiological opinions there certainly was, and, less stridently, many worshipers content to maintain the *status quo* in church design. The high regard in which, clearly, Wallen was held should remind us that not all 1840s Anglicans shared the Ecclesiologists vision of 'a church … as it ought to be',[64] and as historians, we should be cautious lest we legitimise their subjectivity.

Acknowledgements
I am grateful to a number of people who have generously offered assistance in the preparation of this article including: Gwen Brown, Brian Haigh, Hilary Haigh, E. J. Law, Alan Petford and Christopher Tyne. My principal debt is to Diana Burfield.

Abbreviations
ICBS: Incorporated Church Building Society files at Lambeth Palace Library.
WYAS: West Yorkshire Archive Service.

Notes
1   ICBS, 4359. The architect was J. P. Pritchett.
2   *The Ecclesiologist*, 4 (1845), 185. The architect was George Wightwick.
3   ICBS, 4588. The architect was J. T. Fairbank.

4 His birthday is not known, but he was baptised on 26 April 1807 at St Mary, Stepney, London.

5 There is a consensus that he was the William Wallen who died 'in the last quarter of 1853 [in the] City of London' (General Register of Births, Marriages and Deaths, www.gro.gov.uk). However, no notice of his death appears to have been published and Kelly's *Post Office Directory for Yorkshire* (London, 1857), 322, still lists him among the Huddersfield architects, although he is absent from the more or less concurrent *Directory of Leeds and the Woollen District* (Leeds, 1857–8).

6 H. Colvin, *A Biographical Dictionary of British Architects, 1600–1840* (4th ed., New Haven and London, 2008), 1085.

7 A. Felstead *et al.*, *Directory of British Architects 1834–1900* (London, 1993), 509.

8 *Ibid.*, 483.

9 *Dictionary of National Biography* (Oxford, 1890), vol. 28, 408.

10 These are non-conformist chapels in Newbury, Berkshire, 1822 (Colvin, *Dictionary*, 1085), and Newark, Nottinghamshire, 1822–3 (Royal Commission for Historical Monuments, *Nonconformist Chapels and Meeting Houses in Central England* (London, 1986), 159–60).

11 F. H. W. Sheppard (ed.), *Survey of London, Spitalfields* (London, 1957), vol. XXVII, 58.

12 *Robson's London Directory* (London, 1831). The same information appears in the 1835 edition, and in 1836, the name appears on the estimate for substantial repairs to Hawksmoor's Christ Church, Spitalfields, following a fire (*Survey of London*, 167).

13 For Cresy see: D. Burfield, *Edward Cresy 1792–1858, Architect and Civil Engineer* (Donnington, 2003), from which much useful information has been extracted.

14 Burfield, *Cresy*, contains a useful short biography of Taylor (p. 190) as well as many other references to him.

15 *Ibid.*, 77.

16 Taken from M. H. Port, 'Founders of the Royal Institute of British Architects', *Oxford Dictionary of National Biography on-line* (Oxford, 2004–7), www.oxforddnb.com

17 Quoted in Burfield, *Cresy*, 79.

18 The TS is discussed in Burfield, *Cresy*, 169–71. See also *Gentleman's Magazine*, n.s. 6 (1836), 450; n.s. 7 (1837), 57.

19 B. Kaye, *The Development of the Architectural Profession in Britain* (London, 1960), 92.

20 The RIBA Library contains copies of: S. F. Lonard's *Recueil d'architecture* ... (Paris, 1821), 'Presented to the Architectural Society by William Wallen FSA, Member, 3 May 1836'; and F. Melizia, (translated by Mrs E. Cresy), *Lives of Celebrated Architects* ... (1826), 'Presented to the Architectural Society by William Wallen, Dec. 1836'.

21 J. Bettley & N. Pevsner, *The Buildings of England: Essex* (New Haven & London, 2007), 558.

22 W. Wallen, *Little Maplestead* (London, 1836), 145.

23 Indeed, Wallen notes the difficulties in producing the book caused by the absence of 'any records of a parochial nature' at Little Maplestead (p. v). However, the church received some coverage in John Britton, *The Architectural Antiquities of Great Britain* (vol. 1, 1807), 17-18, plus 3 plates.

24 *Ibid.*, 152.

25 For instance on p. 154.

26 *Architectural Magazine,* 3 (1836), 227.

27 Wallen was 29 in 1836 when the book was published, but the 'Address' at the front of the book includes 'So long has elapsed since the announcement of this volume that I feel it incumbent upon me to apologise to my numerous subscribers for the delay' (p. v). It thus seems likely that he would have been soliciting subscriptions some years earlier.

28 This was a curious project. At a time when there were literally thousands of important medieval churches awaiting a thorough, illustrated monograph, it seems

odd that Wallen would choose this church which had, only the year before, received extensive coverage – and no less than ten large plates in W. Caveler, *Select Specimens of Gothic Architecture* (1835). At a time when such books still tended to concentrate on cathedrals, abbeys or Oxbridge colleges, Caveler's treatment of Stone was exceptional.

29 *Gentleman's Magazine*, n.s. 6 (1836), 450.

30 Burfield, *Cresy*, 91–3.

31 The committee meeting of 7 May 1835 received his application (Society of Antiquaries, minute book 36, 488–9, 510).

32 John Bowyer Nichols (1779–1863), a keen antiquary, inherited his father's printing business and editorship of the *Gentleman's Magazine* (Burford, *Cresy*, 187).

33 Peter Frederick Robinson (1776–1858) was a successful architect adept at working in a variety of styles, and the publisher of several books of designs. Robinson would have known Cresy, Taylor and Wallen through the quartet's involvement with the events that surrounded the formation of the Institute of British Architects. For Robinson, *see* Colvin, *Dictionary*, 879–881.

34 In addition, his wife's place of birth is listed as 'Malton, Yorks' in the 1851 census (*ex inf.* E. J. Law). Perhaps news from her family kept the Wallens abreast of the prosperity and building activities in the county.

35 The first reference to him comes on 7 March 1838 (ICBS, 1422).

36 Building the new church at Holmbridge seems to have been beset with problems. A design by Henry Ward, from the early 1830s, was initially chosen, but the work could not be let for the estimated cost. Then in 1837, R. D. Chantrell produced a new design which, despite several revisions, struggled to gain the approval of the ICBS's surveyor. In desperation, the vicar of Almondbury, in whose parish Holmbridge was situated, managed to obtain from the ICBS the Ward drawings 'to which the ICBS seal had already been attached' and promptly gave them to Wallen to execute. It would seem then that Holmbridge was essentially Ward's design, executed by Wallen. Whether Wallen made minor – or possibly major – modifications is not clear, although Holmbridge has much in common with several of Wallen's subsequent churches (ICBS, 1422). Clearly Wallen was waiting in the wings, and might well have moved to Huddersfield somewhat earlier.

37 However, this is a little misleading as seven months earlier, Wallen had written to the ICBS in connection with the Holmbridge project from an address in 'Chapel Hill, Huddersfield'.

38 This is a hand-written statement in the society's minute book 1, 1842–6, 2. The society's archive, in 2009 awaiting cataloguing, is held in the York Minster Library.

39 The paper delivered at York is variously referred to as being on 'The Geometrical Principles of Gothic Architecture' and on 'The Geometrical Principles of Gothic Tracery, whereas the Halifax one was on ' … Gothic Architecture' (*ibid.*).

40 All the information about the society's meetings comes from the first minute book. That for the period 1847–50 is missing, and Wallen is not mentioned as a committee member in the one that covers 1851–7.

41 The society's membership records are patchy (see notes 38 and 40) but from 1850, its annual reports and papers were published systematically in *Associated Architectural Societies Reports and Papers*. The first volume, for 1850, shows Wallen among the YAS members.

42 See P. H. Scholfield, *The Theory of Proportion in Architecture* (Cambridge, 1958), chapter 5; B. G. Morgan, *Canonic Design in English Medieval Architecture* (Liverpool, 1961), 17.

43 Wallen, *Two Essays*, 15.

44 *Ibid*, 5–7.

45 ICBS, file 1422; WYAS, Wakefield, WDP 24.

46 ICBS 2999; WYAS, Leeds, BDP 26/31.

47 ICBS, file 3229; WYAS, Wakefield, WDP 154.

48 WYAS, Bradford, BDP 78.

49 ICBS, file 3024.

50 ICBS, file 3691; WYAS, Wakefield WDP 60.

51 In addition to those things discussed already, Wallen subscribed to most of the parts of G. A. Poole and J. W. Hugall's *The Churches of Yorkshire* (Leeds, 1842–4), the best survey to that date of the county's principal medieval churches.

52 Wallen, *Two Papers*, 7.

53 *Ibid.*, 20.

54 Burfield, *Cresy*, 106–7; 152.

55 Wallen, *Two Essays*, 4.

56 *See* J. M. Crook, *The Architect's Secret* (2003), 84–120.

57 *Leeds Intelligencer*, 5 October 1840.

58 Ibid., 11 October 1845.

59 R. V. Taylor, *The Churches of Leeds* (Leeds, 1875), 51–2.

60 *Ibid.*, 317.

61 In 1833, the Revd W. Carus Wilson designed a new church for Casterton in Cumbria (Westmorland). It was a typical pre-Camdenian, 1830s composition, conceived for a small budget. He published the designs in 1835, yet as late as 1842 Wilson felt it worth re-publishing the plans for the church, along with its specifications 'to show what has recently been done very successfully and at a very moderate expense' and to 'satisfy the many applications which have been made' for the drawings (Wilson, *Helps to the Building of Churches* … (Kirkby Lonsdale, 1842), 13). Clearly he believed that, even at this date, it remained a sound model and it was entirely compatible with Wallen's work of the 1840s; indeed it might well have been the basis for some of it.

62 P. Ahier, *The Story of Three Parish Churches of St Peter the Apostle* (Huddersfield, 1949), 226.

63 I am most grateful to Christopher Tyne for giving me this information.

64 Cambridge Camden Society, *A Few Words to Church Builders* (Cambridge, 1841), 4.

The churches of E. B. Lamb:
an exercise in centralised planning

Anthony Edwards is a practising architect with an interest in the architecture of Lamb extending back many years. He is currently completing a PhD at the University of Liverpool on the man and his work.

IN FEBRUARY 1857, the architect Edward Buckton Lamb (1805–69) gave a lecture at the Architectural Exhibition on 'Architectural Composition'.[1] In it he commented on the many difficulties associated with applying Gothic architecture to the country's 'habitations' and 'public edifices' and also, strangely, to 'our ecclesiastical structures'. But, he fully believed, 'if our associations would allow us, we might overcome' them. At first it seems odd that, not only did he consider that Gothic churches, developed over four hundred years, could still have problems needing solving, but also that he had the solution. He went on to clarify the problem he saw by saying that 'there can be no doubt that the long nave and narrow aisles, divided from each other by numerous columns which screen the minister from the view of his congregation, and also in some degree intercept sound, are inconveniences frequently felt'. He knew that in the new buildings at the time the form was still retained and feared for architects trying anything different, as 'any deviation from such orthodox forms would be pronounced heterodox in the extreme'. But did this deter Lamb? He believed strongly that architecture was a progressive art and that architects should look to the past for ideas and inspiration and rather than copy these they should 'imitate by emulating'.[2] For the previous twelve years he had been designing new churches and experimenting with alternative forms despite the criticisms he received in *The Ecclesiologist* at the time. And did he have the solution? Was there a form he had developed without long naves and numerous columns that gave better sightlines? Today the use of a computer-aided design package allows these statements to be tested to see if they were indeed his intended design principles or simply a later attempt to justify his work.

Methodology

Modern computer programs can be used to design new buildings, but can also be used to help analyse existing buildings. Once buildings have been measured and the structure entered into a computer model it is possible to view it in many different ways, suppressing parts by type or usage, changing the level of detail or scale, or altering the viewing position. This provides the opportunity of interrogating the model in ways that are impossible to do with the building itself. A clearer picture of the design and construction is made possible, highlighting particular areas of detail and leading to a greater understanding of both the architect's concept and its practical application.

One such area for study in Lamb's churches is the relationship of the seating for the congregation, the pulpit and the structure and in particular the influence of the internal columns. For Lamb and his Low Church clients it was the pulpit which formed the key focus for the building rather than the altar and a clear view from as many seats as possible was vital in allowing people to see and hear the preacher.

Lamb was born in 1805 and this makes him much older than the leading Gothic Revivalist architects who were practising at the same time as him and this age difference is crucial to the understanding of Lamb's work. His education was complete by the time that A. W. N. Pugin (1812–52) and the Cambridge Camden Society laid down their doctrinaire principles. In 1828 he completed his articles with Lewis Nockalls Cottingham (1787–1847), among the first nineteenth-century church restorers who endeavoured to achieve archeologically correct work. Lamb began to practise architecture following the Picturesque principles of composition and materials. He continued to do during the twelve years he also worked with John Claudius Loudon (1783–1843) the horticulturist, architect and critic whose principal illustrator he was from 1831 to 1843 assisting him with the architectural work of his landscaping projects of cemeteries and parks.

The first attempt
It was following his work with Loudon that in 1845 Lamb's patron, Sir Robert Frankland Russell (1784–1849), secured him a scheme for a church in the small hamlet of Healey in North Yorkshire. This was Lamb's first significant church. St Paul's was built for Admiral Lord Harcourt who lived in the nearby village of Swinton and the church Lamb designed shows a plan form with little change from those which other architects of the day were using but were from the plans that were to come later in his career.

The plan is a Latin cross and this was one of only two churches where Lamb adopted this simple form without endeavouring to create a new one. The nave is a simple rectangle of 40ft x 17ft 4in and the chancel a rectangle of 22ft x 15ft separated by the 10ft-wide crossing from which there are two identically sized 10ft x 8ft transepts with part of the northern one set aside for a vestry. Lamb completes the traditional form with a tower over the crossing and a porch at the south-west corner of the nave. The smallness of the church allows Lamb to cover the nave and chancel without the need for any internal columns by using a scissor-truss roof, albeit with additional elaborate braces. Any restrictions on the view of the preacher from the pews is therefore only from the supports for the nave, chancel and transept arches.

St Paul's was supported by a grant from the Incorporated Church Building Society (ICBS) and records exist at Lambeth Palace Library of Lamb's original seating layout including the seats allocated for both adults and children.[3] Once the church has been measured, the structure entered accurately into a computer model and the internal pews, pulpit, reading desk, and other fittings added, it is then a simple task to add the relevant number of people in their positions, assuming between 18 and 20ins width per seat, to ascertain the success of his church planning in his new forms without having to resort physically to filling the church with people. It is now possible to show all seats which have a clear view of the preacher with a shaded area, highlighting those seats outside this area whose view is obscured (Fig. 1). Out of the 275

Fig. 1: Healey, St Paul, North Yorkshire, 1845–8. Lamb's original layout of 1847 showing only a 93% success in terms of viewing lines before Lamb revised the layout bringing all seating forward into the nave.

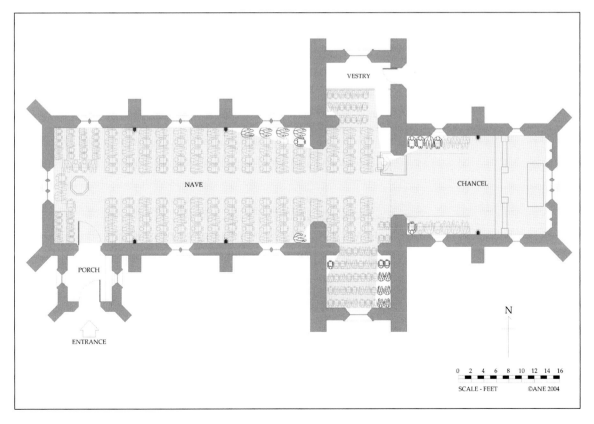

total seats, including 14 in the chancel, only 11 adults and 9 children are without a clear view giving a 93% success rate. In fact the layout shown by Lamb was not the one eventually used and the pulpit was moved from the side of the chancel arch to be in front of the nave arch, the vestry enlarged to take up the whole of the north transept and all the seating in the south transept for the children gave way for the organ. The seating in the chancel was doubled and all the seating beneath the crossing removed. This new layout now meant that 100% of the nave seats had a clear view, although the first two rows on the south side are in front of the preacher and only 16 seats of the 28 in the chancel have an obstructed view. In Lamb's original design it was the nave wall line, which continued into the crossing while in the church as built, it was the chancel wall line that was followed creating a narrower seating area. No working drawings exist to show whether this was an intended alteration following the initial design or poor setting out on site. Lamb certainly began his career with a church with a well-planned seating layout, even if there was a huge reduction of 102 seats compared to the initial design. The majority of the reduction was in the seat allocation of the children, which dropped from 99 to only 25, and Lamb may simply have overestimated the requirements for accommodating the juveniles in the area.

Controversy begins

While St Paul's, Healey, was under construction Lamb began the design for his next church – Holy Trinity, Prestwood in Buckinghamshire built between 1847 and 1849. Here he was required to accommodate a similar-sized congregation, which he achieved by the addition of a north and south aisle for the whole length of the nave. The chancel abuts the nave directly with no crossing or transepts. There is also no tower and the bell is housed in a turret over the west end, thickened in the centre to support it. Beyond this to the west, Lamb added a large, 14ft-square extension to form a baptistery. Such a strange addition was a controversial feature that caused much consternation in the review in *The Ecclesiologist* in April 1848. 'We must express our dissatisfaction …The chapel has a chancel at each end, – seriously: at least we cannot otherwise explain the design … the chapel is most unsuccessful'.[4]

The ICBS also thought 'the chancel like appearance of the projection at the west end of the nave is to be regretted' and suggested that 'surely the effect of the base of a future tower would be preferable to this unusual feature' giving the building a more traditional form when fully completed.[5] The nave is quite narrow and at 15ft 6in almost 2ft narrower than that at Healey so only a braced scissor-truss is required again, but this time in its simplest form and at a high level to allow for a clerestory above the shallow monopitched aisle roofs. The addition of the two aisles meant that to gain access to them from the nave it was necessary to use the normal method and form arches in this division wall, thus introducing four columns into the design. The only other possible viewing restrictions of the preacher are the chancel and nave arches and the internal buttresses needed to help support the bell-turret.

A signed plan by Lamb dated 1849 exists showing the intended seating layout for a total of 241 sittings.[6] An analysis of the viewing lines shows that out of the 39 seats with an obstructed view, all but six are due to the introduction of the four columns thus reducing the 'success' of the plan to only 84% (Fig. 2). A grant for this church was also requested from the ICBS, where records show that an earlier scheme for 281 sittings was first envisaged. Unfortunately no plan survives of this layout and although pew lengths, numbers and positions in the church are indicated on the society's Form B numerous attempts to ascertain the layout have

Fig. 2: Prestwood, Holy Trinity, Buckinghamshire, 1848–9. Viewing layout showing the restrictions associated with the introduction of aisles and columns. Based on a plan in the Centre for Buckinghamshire Studies.

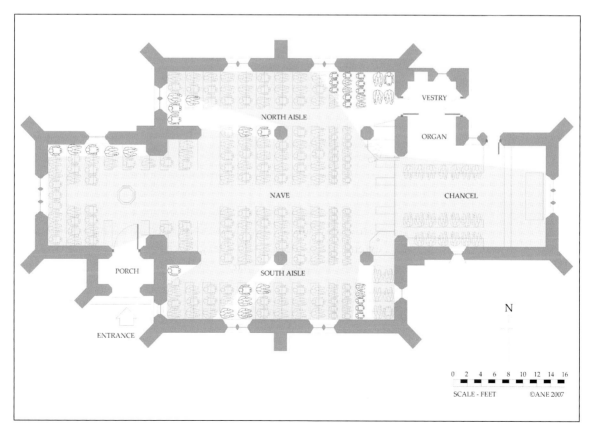

not been successful.[7] All the pews were entirely rebuilt and re-spaced in 1920 and the total number of sittings was further reduced to 195, which is its capacity today.[8] The original timber floor to the pews, however, was not replaced and there are a few tantalisingly small areas of timber remaining where the original pews were cut off at floor level. An analysis of this surviving evidence of the original pews indicates that the pew layout installed was not that of the 1849 layout, but unfortunately there are not enough of the original pews remaining to ascertain what this layout might have been.

Viewing success improves

Lamb's next ecclesiastical project was a chapel at the Brompton Hospital for Consumption and Diseases of the Chest in London, 1849–50.[9] The chapel of St Luke was added when Sir Henry Foulis (1800–1870), who was the rector of Great Brickhill in Buckinghamshire, paid for its erection as a memorial to his recently deceased sister, Sofia Francis Paunceforte Duncombe. At this chapel Lamb reverted to the simpler traditional plan form with a large rectangular nave 60ft x 24ft and a chancel 26ft 6in x 14ft with two bay-ended transepts, only 16ft 8in wide by 8ft deep. This was Lamb's widest church to date and he chose to use a hammer-beam roof, thus following the lead of his medieval forebears when wider spans were required. Lamb was always striving to progress architecture and rather than use a single hammer-beam with a crown-post roof above the hammer posts, he used a scissor-truss and not at the higher level to replace the crown post, but at the lower level of the hammer-beam. Lamb thus creates an entirely new form by superimposing two traditional ones and which was described disparagingly by *The Ecclesiologist* as 'a chaos of carpentry so near our heads we have seldom seen'.[10]

Again, there are no internal columns with the viewing restrictions arising only from the supports for the two arches to the two transepts, as the chancel arch is the full width of the chancel. Because of the site relationship of the chapel to the hospital, Lamb was able to accommodate the other remaining requirements of porch, vestry and bell-tower as a separate entity to the south of the chapel to form part of a long corridor linking the chapel to the central wing of the hospital.

Lamb created a seating plan where all the seats were located in the nave with just a small row of five seats each, on either side of the chancel for the hospital dignitaries. No seats were placed in the two transepts either, which were quite small and predominantly used as a circulation space and the south transept contains a memorial window to Sofia. The sightlines for seats in the nave to the pulpit are uninterrupted, as are those to the south side of the chancel. There are only five seats on the north side of the chancel with no view of the preacher and of the 168 seats in total in the channel, 97% therefore have a clear view or 100% of the 158 seats in the nave.

The traditional plan highlights the problem

In March 1849, Lamb's patron Sir Robert Frankland Russell died and was buried with his ancestors at the family seat of Thirkleby Park, North Yorkshire.[11] His widow, Lady Louisa (1790–1871), employed Lamb to build a memorial church to her late husband on the site of the existing Georgian church. Lamb was somewhat constrained in his design for All Saints by having to leave the Frankland vault undisturbed. Perhaps also with a desire to impress Lady Frankland Russell with a view to retaining her as his client, he produced one of his most orthodox church plans. A long nave of 48ft 6in with a width of 17ft 8in is joined to a 25ft x 15ft chancel whose size is determined by the Frankland vault below. To the south of the chancel and to its full-length, is the Frankland Aisle leading to the small Frankland Chapel, while to the north is a small vestry. The nave has a 7ft 6in wide aisle on each side, with that to the south running the full length of the nave. The aisle to the north is cut short at the west end by the intrusion of the porch and a small internal lobby area leading to the base of the tall tower at the north-west corner which houses the font. This is the only area on the plan where Lamb introduced a somewhat unusual, though highly logical and practical variation, to what otherwise is an arrangement which can be seen in many parish churches in England. The nave here is narrower than at Brompton but Lamb chose to use the same hammer-beam roof principle again, this time without any scissor-truss form, relying on a simple collar at high-level and a large brace-arch beginning at the internal end of the hammer-beam and finishing below the collar. There are then, in effect, no hammer posts and the roof is more of the false hammer-beam type, although the remaining features added by Lamb create yet another new form.

As at Prestwood, Lamb introduced a series of arches and columns in the division walls between aisles and nave. There are four columns for the south aisle, but only three for the north due to the arrangement of the porch and tower. The only other remaining restriction for sight lines are the supports to the chancel arch which are minimal as the arch is made as wide as possible.

The seating plan at Thirkleby, has all 183 seats in the nave and two aisles with none in the chancel and therefore all are in front of the pulpit. This is again placed to the north side of the chancel arch. The introduction of the seven columns has a detrimental impact on the viewing with seats for 10 adults and 4 children having interrupted views, but with only three of the columns creating these problems Lamb still achieves a 92% success rate.

A column is born

At the same time as Thirkleby, All Saints, Lamb was commissioned by Lady Frankland Russell to build a chapel of ease on part of her estate at Blubberhouses, North Yorkshire some twenty miles to the south-west. With no requirement to seat a large congregation, Lamb's scheme consists of a rectangular nave, 40ft x 17ft 3in and a short chancel of 16ft 3in x 13ft, with a small vestry to the south. A narrow north aisle of only 4ft 6in runs two thirds of the nave to accommodate the font, with the tower base adjacent and next to this the porch at the far north-west corner. These four spaces then make up a larger rectangle of 40ft x 23ft 6in internally creating Lamb's simplest and most regular external outline. The nave width is 17ft 3in, only 3 inches narrower than that at Healey, but rather than using a simple scissor truss he chooses to take this scissor-truss principle and create his own variation. Lamb moves the crossing points of the two scissor rafters to immediately below the collar and then uses a two-piece king-post, with one piece each side of the truss bolted through the crossing point and at the ridge, to create a new truss form. Timber sizes for the main truss are made from 6in by 8in timbers and appear very heavy and oversized for a roof of such a relatively short span. However, due to the roof finish of stone slabs up to 2in thick as well as the church being in an area of the country with heavy winter snowfalls, Lamb may well have simply chosen to be overcautious in his design (Fig. 3).

The wall between the nave and the north aisle is completely removed and the space is spanned by a wall-plate acting as a beam supporting the nave roof and assisted by a single column placed at mid-span. The location of the column also supports one of the two principal trusses to the nave. The column has a stone corbel on each face; one to support the roof truss, two to support timber braces for the wall plate/beam and one to support the roof timbers of the aisle roof. This configuration of a corbel on each face of a column supporting timber work may well have sparked an idea that was to become a key feature of many of the Lamb's later churches as we will see later (Fig. 4).

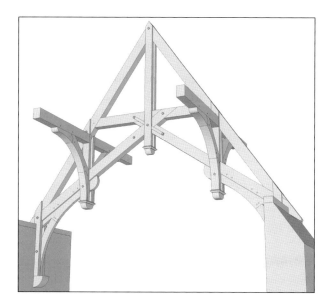

Fig. 3: Blubberhouses, St Andrew, North Yorkshire, 1849–51. Close-up view of computer model of principal nave truss showing Lamb's variation on the scissor truss.

Fig. 4: Blubberhouses, 1849–51. Single column dividing the nave from the north aisle and the possible inspiration for the columns of the central space in his later churches.

The single column is therefore the only restriction to the sightlines to the pulpit and views to the chancel are greatly increased with only minimal supports to the chancel arch. In his seating layout, all the 113 seats are confined to the nave, where in fact the pews from the old Georgian church at Thirkleby are re-used. All seats are in front of the pulpit that this time is located to the south of the chancel arch rather than the north. This is possibly due to the location of the vestry on the south side of the chancel placed here by Lamb to make full use of the higher part of the sloping site. There is no interruption to sightlines due to the single column as the north aisle is given over solely to the font and for the first time there is a success rate of 100% visibility.

The 'Latin-Quadrate cross' plan appears

Shortly after the completion of St Andrew's, Blubberhouses, Lamb was working on his third church for Lady Frankland Russell on another of her estates at Aldwark, North Yorkshire. St Stephen's, was built between 1851 and 1853 and is one of Lamb's most important churches. He took on board the new trend of polychromy, inspired by William Butterfield at All Saints', Margaret Street, London, which was designed in 1849 and under construction at the time, creating a church of stone, brick and pebbles with coloured tile diaper patterning in the roof.

The single pier from Blubberhouses is used four times to create a large central space where the four columns divide the central space into nine smaller spaces. Lamb has effectively used a Quadrate cross (Fig. 5), but then superimposed a larger Latin cross to give a shorter arm for the chancel and a longer arm for the nave. The combination of these two crosses provides Lamb with a

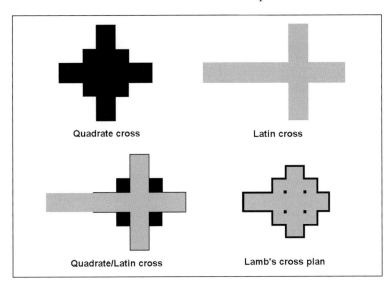

Quadrate cross   Latin cross

Quadrate/Latin cross   Lamb's cross plan

Fig. 5: Variants on the cross plan.

new form: the Latin cross giving the more traditional long nave and short chancel while the Quadrate cross at the crossing allows a larger centralised area nearer the pulpit. In the resultant form, the barriers between the crossing and the nave, and the nave and the transepts, are now more fluid and freely expressed. The chancel is Lamb's first where it is wider than it is long and is so small that it only has space for the altar. The pulpit and reading desk positions are brought forward from the chancel arch and into this new central space

There are short north and south transepts and these are based on the bay shapes he had used a few years earlier at Brompton Hospital Chapel, London. The tower is to the north-west and almost isolated from the church, joined to the main building only by a small circulation space with a door in each wall. This space provides a route for the congregation into the nave using two of the doors and for the vicar using the other two doors because the vestry is under the tower. The plan does not allow a separate vestry to be added to any part of the east end of the church successfully so Lamb used the last remaining available space.

The nave width at Aldwark is again rather narrow at only 17ft and a simple double collar principal truss is used with a single king-post and arched braces below. The transepts use a similar roof design and as they are 2ft narrower the purlins are below those of the nave, allowing the lower purlins to meet those of their counterparts in the nave in a simple pin joint at the crossing. The four columns introduced have minimal effect on the viewing lines with only four seats in the north transept being obstructed due to the column nearest the pulpit. All the other 123 seats situated under the crossing, nave and in the south transept have clear sightlines giving another high success rate at 97% (Fig. 6).

The new plan develops

Lamb began working on two larger versions of this new centralised design at about the same time at opposite ends of the country; his revised scheme of Christ Church, West Hartlepool, Co. Durham, built in 1852–4 and his rebuilding scheme of St Margaret's, Leiston, Suffolk, 1853–4. Both churches take the Quadrate cross form with a larger Latin cross superimposed as used at Aldwark, but the four corner spaces of the central nine spaces are now each large enough a form to serve as more than mere circulation spaces (Fig. 8). They either become additional seating areas or spaces for the organ, vestry or baptistery. At West Hartlepool the central space is now 60ft 9in long by 62ft 4in wide compared to the 27ft long by 31ft wide at Aldwark, but at Leiston

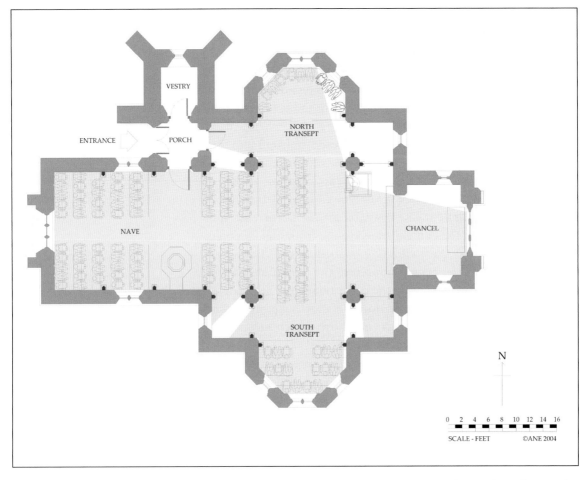

VESTRY

ENTRANCE PORCH

NORTH
TRANSEPT

NAVE

CHANCEL

SOUTH
TRANSEPT

N

0 2 4 6 8 10 12 14 16
SCALE - FEET   ©ANE 2004

Fig. 6: Aldwark, St Stephen, North Yorkshire, 1851–3. Viewing layout showing initial success of a centralised plan with only four sittings unable to see the preacher.

the east-west length becomes longer at 54ft 2in than the north-south width of 51ft 6in, giving more dominance to the principal axis of the church. Also for the first time, the four columns of the crossing form a perfect square compared with West Hartlepool and Aldwark where the width between columns across the nave was wider than that across the transepts giving more emphasis to the north-south axis.

Both churches also have short transepts to each side of the church, although they are square with gables rather than with a hipped polygonal-ended bay. The naves are longer and 28ft wide, finishing in a tall square tower centrally placed at the west end. At Leiston, this tower was the thirteenth-century original which had to be retained when the original very long and thin church was rebuilt and its location may have influenced Lamb's design at West Hartlepool. He also continued in both churches with short chancels, not large enough for any seating, with that at Leiston only 12ft 6in deep. However, the pulpit is brought out in front of the chancel arch and well into the central space, placing it adjacent

AS BUILT - VIEWING INCLUDING CHANCEL				
		Seats	Viewing	
Church-by date	Total	Obstructed	success	Columns
Healey	173	16	90.8%	0
Prestwood	195	23	88.2%	4
Blubberhouses	113	0	100.0%	1
Brompton	168	5	97.0%	0
Thirkleby	183	14	92.3%	7
Aldwark	127	4	96.9%	4
Leiston	814	20	97.5%	4
Englefield Green	320	5	98.4%	0
West Hartlepool	904	35	96.1%	4
Castle Douglas	134	0	100.0%	0
Bagby	183	4	97.8%	0
Gospel Oak	681	8	98.8%	4
TOTALS	**3995**	**134**	**96.6%**	**28**

Table 1: Viewing success for all twelve churches as built including chancel.

churches giving an average of only a little over two per church. During the twenty-year period Lamb had slowly and steadily refined his plans to provide churches with both a central space and minimal columns allowing as many of the congregation as possible to see and hear clearly the sermons preached from the pulpit. But such a form did have its drawbacks. Computers are calculating machines and the computer models created for each church allow the internal areas of the different functions to be determined. The relationship between the areas of seating and the areas of circulation needed in order to be able to reach that seating can be assessed (Table 2). Despite the emphasis on a large centralised space and a short nave, a high percentage of the floor

AS BUILT - SEATING v CIRCULATION INCLUDING CHANCEL			
	Areas in square inches		Seating
Church-by date	Total	Seating	area
Healey	161280	85560	53.1%
Prestwood	218764	127245	58.2%
Blubberhouses	121398	58449	48.1%
Brompton	291180	143806	49.4%
Thirkleby	292250	124216	42.5%
Aldwark	201566	80292	39.8%
Leiston	614888	418482	68.1%
Englefield Green	343909	206204	60.0%
West Hartlepool	683951	475284	69.5%
Castle Douglas	181908	86423	47.5%
Bagby	173411	115760	66.8%
Gospel Oak	882252	452633	51.3%
TOTALS	**4166757**	**2374354**	**57.0%**

Table 2: Seating v. circulation for all twelve churches as built including chancel.

area is required for circulation, something that is not obviously apparent from the plans. Over the twelve churches it works out that on average a little under half the internal space is not available for the congregation to sit in.

When Lamb took his design principle of a central space to larger churches he created other problems. The disposal of the surface water from the necessarily vast roofs became more and more difficult. Many of his churches were designed with internal rain water pipes hidden within the structure of the walls, unfortunately leading to the inevitable damp problems as they deteriorated and subsequently leaked with age. The roofing of these large internal spaces however, did lead to some most impressive timber constructions and were a deliberate attempt to create variations on traditional roof design. Every roof structure for these twelve new churches was different. There is always something of interest in the design whether it is the overall roof type Lamb used as a starting point or the number of collars, vertical ties, braces or purlins. He used the standard sized timbers of the day, with the tried and tested pegged mortise, tenon and lapped joints, but supplemented this with modern bolts and plates to create new forms. Lamb was striving to achieve his main objective as stated in 1846 in his book *Studies of Ancient Domestic Architecture*, that architects should imitate by emulating.

Now that all the twelve churches are available, comparative plans that identify the areas of main seating, secondary seating, transepts, tower, porch and chancel can be studied to see any development in their size, shape and relationship or any common themes (Fig. 10). At first it seems that the only consistency is the fact that the chancel is in the usual place at the east end with the main seating space to its west; even Lamb had to follow this orthodoxy, while it seems he was quite content to move the position of the tower to virtually any compass point. But a closer study reveals that there has been a steady change over the twenty years from an entrance at the west end and a longer route through a rectangular preaching space, to a central entrance and a shorter processional route through a squarer central preaching space. Lamb had indeed followed the design statements in his lecture of 1857 in both the nine churches in the preceding twelve years and the three churches in the eight years that followed. Lamb had a fundamental belief that architecture was a progressive art and he saw any rules laid down for the planning of churches more as guidelines, allowing him freedom to experiment with the form without destroying the function in his desire to create new church forms.

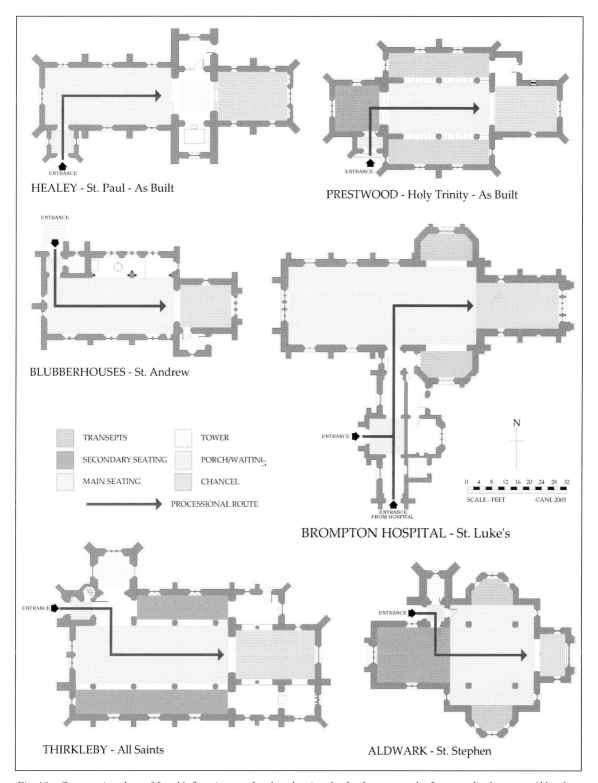

Fig. 10: Comparative plans of Lamb's first six new churches showing the development to the first centralised space at Aldwark in 1851–3.

Today's computer-aided design software provides a valuable tool to help understand Lamb's buildings; to see the success of the planning when creating a central preaching space for worship and maximising the number of seats with a view of the preacher and to see how problems were solved, such as the removal of rainwater and the spanning of large areas. This type of detailed analysis of these churches, is leading to a greater understanding of this unusual and quirky, but clever, man, the architect, Edward Buckton Lamb.

Notes

1 E. B. Lamb, 'Architectural Composition', lecture delivered at the Architectural Exhibition on 3 February, 1857, and published in full in *Building News*, 20 February 1857, 185.

2 E. B. Lamb, *Studies of Ancient Domestic Architecture* (London, 1846), 1.

3 Signed plan, 15 May 1847, ICBS 3522.

4 *The Ecclesiologist*, 8 (1848), 320.

5 Report on scheme by ICBS architect, ICBS 3941, item 18 in file.

6 Signed plan, 1849, Centre for Buckinghamshire Studies, Aylesbury, PR168A/3/4.

7 Form B, ICBS 3941, item 9 in file.

8 Desmond Keen, *Prestwood Parish Church: A Short History of Holy Trinity Church* (church guide, 1997), 20.

9 'The Brompton Hospital Estate', *Survey of London, vol. XLI, Southern Kensington: Brompton* (London, 1983), 135–9.

10 *The Ecclesiologist*, 11 (1850), 196.

11 *The Builder*, 12 October 1850, 485–6.

12 Ibid., 2 September 1854, 462.

13 The photograph is displayed in the gallery of the church, which has now been deconsecrated and converted to the Hartlepool Art Gallery.

14 *The Builder, 2 September 1854, 462*

15 'Architectural Room at the Royal Academy', *The Ecclesiologist*, 16 (1855), 150.

16 Richard Falkner, *Church and School in Englefield Green* (church guide printed by Brian Hooker, 1973), 6.

17 Form B, ICBS 5323, items 3 and 4.

18 This figure increases by only 0.5% to 97.2% if the chancel is excluded as some of Lamb's churches do have seats in their chancels.

'The callous Mr Christian': the making and unmaking of a professional reputation

Martin Cherry

EWAN CHRISTIAN (1814–95) – vice-president, and Royal Gold Medallist of the RIBA, architect to the Ecclesiastical Commission (along with many other public posts), and with over 2,000 works to his name – has had a bad press.[1] Throughout the twentieth century he was routinely dismissed as boring. He suffered, as did almost all his contemporaries, from the visceral reaction to all things Victorian that did not really begin to dispel until the early 1960s. More specifically, he shared the fate of those Victorian architects who had very large practices, produced phenomenal quantities of work and sometimes found it difficult to keep a level quality. Basil Clarke thought that only the hyperactive Scott was duller.[2] Much of Christian's work, especially for the Ecclesiastical Commission, was done on a tight budget and can appear off-the-shelf and unimaginative. Given a free rein, however, he could produce outstanding and original designs, often with a distinctive and austere aesthetic, such as St Mark's, Leicester, considered by many to be his masterpiece (Fig. 1). Yet, Christian has never been admitted to the pantheon of Victorian architects, despite the fact that he rose to the very peak of his profession – and stayed there. Significantly, the seeds from which his poor reputation grew were sown during his lifetime. As a committed Evangelical who was deeply engaged in the works of the erastian Ecclesiastical Commission, the High Church and Anglo-Catholics treated him with suspicion. As an active institutional reformer and committee man, he was not trusted by those who objected to attempts to regulate the profession and who saw architecture as a fine art. Since, for much of the twentieth century, critics assessed ecclesiastical architecture through the prism of High-Church aesthetics and the canons of fine art, Christian's reputation was destined for a rough ride.

The critical legacy

The influential architectural critics, Nikolaus Pevsner and Ian Nairn, seldom pulled their punches. Christian's restorations were the object of particular venom. Of St Peter's, Shelford, Nottinghamshire, Pevsner remarked that it was 'So ruthlessly restored by the callous Mr Christian in 1876–8 that little remains for enjoyment'.[3] Similarly, 'Do not be put off by the horrible

Martin Cherry was Head of Listing and then Research Director at English Heritage. He is now an independent researcher and edits the journal Vernacular Architecture. His publications and research interests range from medieval history to nineteenth-century architecture and present-day conservation policy.

49

Fig. 1: Leicester, St Mark, 1870–72, a gift to the town from W. Perry Herrick of Beaumanor Park, a major local benefactor of church-building. It is considered by many to be Christian's finest church. (English Heritage/NMR BB93/29289)

restoration of 1867 by Ewan Christian which has left the outside maimed and valueless, the hard windows stamped into the walls with real hatred', wrote Nairn of St Mary's, Aldingbourne in West Sussex – with real hatred.[4] Throughout the influential *Buildings of England* series, Pevsner and his collaborators dismissed Christian's restorations as 'destructive', 'hard and rebuffing', 'dreadful', 'restored out of existence', or at best 'dull', 'drab', and 'routine'. Such assessments extended to Christian's new churches, especially in the earlier volumes. Judgements such as 'entirely indifferent'; 'unexceptional'; 'dull inside as well as outside', and 'really of no interest' reinforced the expectation that 'typically Christian' was a yardstick of Victorian mediocrity. The effects of this invective were insidious. Coming at a time when Victorian architecture was beginning to undergo serious reappraisal, not least by Pevsner and Nairn themselves, vituperative criticism from authorities deemed to be sympathetic to the age could be especially damaging, if only in that it created a resistance to look afresh at Christian's works.

This negative assessment of Christian served to reinforce the received opinion of earlier twentieth-century critics. As we have seen, Basil Clarke thought that his churches never rose above the mediocre.[5] Other key writers – Kenneth Clark and Goodhart-Rendel, for instance – simply ignored him. To a certain extent, this view still remains widespread. 'Little of his immense output shows imagination' or an architect in the 'mass production league' are typical verdicts, what might be called a consensus view of the architect.[6] Yet, the later twentieth-century critical legacy is strangely ambivalent. Pevsner found St Olave's, Stoke Newington (north London) 'generally pleasant considering its designer'[7] and there are numerous other occasions throughout the *Buildings of England* series where Pevsner is taken by surprise at Christian's ability to dent his own prejudices. Wickham Bishops, Essex, is 'quite ambitious' while Kenilworth in Warwickshire is 'spacious … vigorous' (Fig. 2); the tower of Christ Church, Forest Hill (Lewisham, south London) is 'handsome' and the broach spire at Leyland (Lancashire), 'excellently outlined'. Cumulatively, both Pevsner's and other historians' assessments of individual churches begin to throw a more nuanced light on Christian's output, one that is more consistent with most contemporary views of the architect.

Writers of synthetic studies of Victorian architecture placed him more securely in his context and were better able to judge his significance. Christian emerges prominently within a small band of architects who widened the range of the Ecclesiological

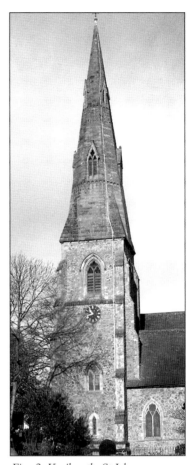

Fig. 2: Kenilworth, St John, Warwickshire, 1851–2, one of many churches by Christian that confounded critics conditioned to think of him as pedestrian. (Author)

Fig. 3: Staverton, St Paul de Leon, Devon, restored 1873–82, showing Christian's 'very wilful plate tracery on the south side'. (Author)

movement's repertoire. Stefan Muthesius noted his 'strong tendency to massiveness and horizontality and also towards the integration of tracery into the wall' (Fig. 3).[8] Peter Anson recognised his contribution to the development in the 1850s of a 'very different type of church', a variant of Ecclesiological correctness more attuned to Evangelical worship.[9] Christian's place among the progressives of the Gothic Revival, at least during the 1840s and 1850s, was recognised by contemporaries. Eastlake, whose *History of the Gothic Revival* appeared 'at the zenith of the revivalist movement', considered Christian to be among a small band of architects (Carpenter, Scott, Hadfield, T. H. Wyatt, David and Raphael Brandon, Pearson and J. C. Buckler were the others) who reinvigorated the style, moving away from copyism 'with more intelligence and with a better sense of adaptation [and] laid the foundation for a more scholarlike treatment'.[10] Eastlake draws a distinction between Christian and others such as Joseph Clarke, Teulon and J. H. Hakewill, who followed in the footsteps of Scott 'with [a] more or less tendency to individual peculiarities', and 'a certain number of younger men' – Street, Woodyer, White and Bodley – who 'showed an early inclination to strike out in a new line for themselves', influenced by continental precedents.[11]

What Eastlake saw as the beginning of a generational divide could be expressed in terms of conservatism, on the one hand, and imaginative innovation, on the other. Put yet another way,

Christian's buildings were described in a memoir published shortly after his death as being 'distinguished more for quietness and repose than for architectural effect, although they are by no means wanting in that'.[12] *The Ecclesiologist*, ever on the lookout for Low Church deviation, at first gave him the benefit of the doubt. His proposals to restore St Mary's, Scarborough (1848–52), while far from perfect, were approached 'in a very proper spirit', being informed by a scrupulous analysis of the medieval fabric.[13] The journal's judgement on Christian's new church, St Stephen's, Tonbridge, Kent (1851–4) is illuminating: 'This church, though not without merit of a certain kind in its architectural features, is a miserable specimen of bad ritual arrangement'.[14]

Fig. 4: Douglas, St Thomas, Isle of Man, 1849. The first Manx church to embody ecclesiological principles. Christian's family came from the Isle of Man and his cousin was archdeacon there. J. M. Neale found it 'unworthy of description'. (From an original drawing by Christian, Manx National Heritage, MS 09432/2)

The core of the issue, identified by Anson, was the challenge of integrating Evangelical requirements into a mainstream aesthetic moulded by the High Church. This is what Christian did well, as sensitive critics have appreciated. John Newman recognised the importance of his first church (St John's, Hildenborough, 1843–4) (Figs. 5a & b), 'internally of startling power', dominated by 'the tremendous arch-braced roofs … Christian's intention is clear – he has rethought the problem of the preaching church, to create a broad central space, which makes the galleries of the Commissioners' churches no longer necessary'.[15] The mature version was summed up perceptively by Julian Orbach in his account of St Matthew's, Cheltenham (1878) (Fig. 6): 'a fascinating church, sternly detailed outside and inside, a very broad nave canted at the [east] end to a narrow chancel, giving the maximum space for the congregation as the Evangelical wing of the Anglican Church liked, but in the High Victorian dress more usual for ritualistic or High Church congregations.'[16]

'A life of independent service, not of exploits'[17]

A number of qualities underpinned Christian's professional success. Among them were his skill and accuracy in architectural drawing, his powers of close observation and attention to detail that were noted by observers throughout his life and formed part of what *The Ecclesiologist* understood as 'the proper spirit' in his Scarborough proposals. Whilst articled to Matthew Habershon, from 1829, he had provided sketches for *The Ancient Half-Timbered Houses of England* (1836) that 'far surpassed [Habershon's] expectations'.[18] He later assisted William Railton on the competition drawings for the Houses of Parliament.[19] Christian's only book, produced at one of those rare moments when business was slack, focussed on a single church, Skelton, North Yorkshire, and served to advertise his wares as architectural draughtsman and analyst (Fig. 7).[20]

Another key quality was his mastery of constructional detail and a preparedness to explore innovative solutions, not least in resolving complex planning problems on awkward sites. Christian cut his teeth on the practical building side as a site supervisor from 1836 to 1841 for the Norwich architect, John Brown. He later developed a 'reputation for judgment and experience' regarding major structural failure, and his advice was sought by such as George Gilbert Scott. At Alconbury, Cambridgeshire, he rebuilt the distressed lower stage of the medieval tower whilst supporting

Figs. 5 a & b: Hildenborough, St John, Kent, 1843–4. Christian's first church with a powerful interior dominated by its remarkable arch-braced roof. (Geoff Brandwood)

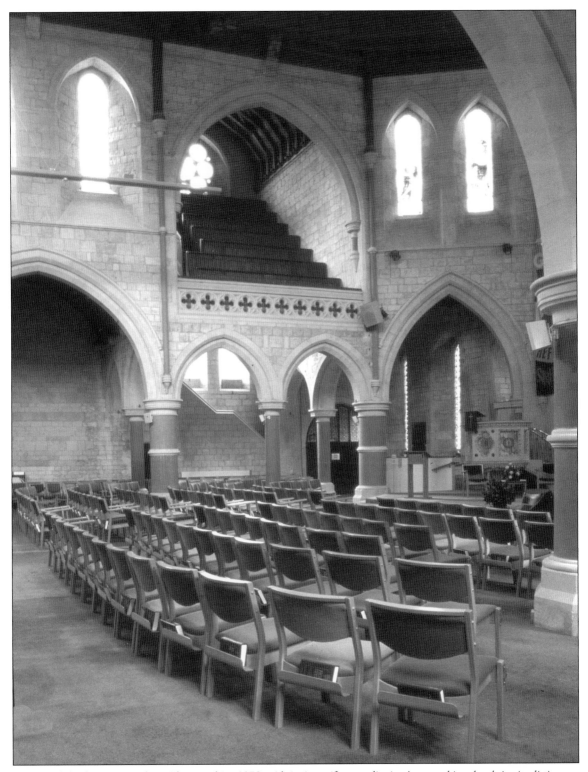

Fig. 6: Cheltenham, St Matthew, Gloucestershire, 1878, with its 'magnificent auditorium', a preaching church in ritualistic dress. Christian's low reputation eased the way for the removal of its steeple in 1952, tower in 1972 and drastic internal reordering (1999). (Author)

Fig. 7: Illustration of St Giles, Skelton, North Yorkshire, from Christian's only published book Architectural Illustrations of Skelton Church, Yorkshire *of 1846 that served to broadcast his skills as an architectural draughtsman.*

the upper stage intact on a massive timber framework – 'a hazardous but successful operation'.[21] But his confidence in his own opinions ruffled feathers, especially when making *ex cathedra* decisions as the Ecclesiastical Commission's architect. Butterfield was so incensed by Christian's demands regarding the thickness of the walls for one of his plans, that 'he would have given up the church altogether rather than concede the point.'[22] On the occasion of the Royal Gold Medal award, the RIBA president, Edward I'Anson recounted one occasion when he had differed from the views of Christian and, 'though he felt he was right, he admired [Christian's] sense of duty to his employers [that is the Commission] and thought at the time "well done thou good and faithful servant"' – not, it might be observed, an effusive compliment.[23] Christian's tendency not to yield a point is comically illustrated by his determination, as a minority of one, to

Figs. 8a & b: Contrary to received
opinion, Christian was a careful and
sensitive restorer who took great pains
to understand and respect the original
fabric.
a: (this page) Austrey, St Nicholas,
Warwickshire, 1844–5
b: (opposite page) Warkworth, St
Laurence, Northumberland, 1860.
(Author)

build a full-size mock up of a proposed new organ in order to
prove that is was inappropriately scaled.[24] But any impression that
Christian was closed to new ideas is dispelled not least by his
reactions to America. After a trip there in later life: 'no-one can
pass through any city in America without learning at every step.'
He was impressed by the 'go-aheadness' of the place where
inventions connected with building were 'straightway adopted all
over the country until something better was produced, when that,
in its turn, was taken up.'[25]

The key post held by Christian, one that made him, *par
excellence*, an establishment figure, was that of consultant architect
to the Ecclesiastical Commission, which he held from 1851 until
his death. It was one of many – chairman of the ICBS committee
of architects (from 1869; he joined the committee in 1849),
architect to the Charities Commission (1887) to name but two –
but it was the one that turned some of the artistic and High
Church establishment against him. Christian saw his road to

advancement as having been via a number of key commissions.[26] According to an annotated list of works he compiled himself, Hildenborough was his 'first church won in competition'. The restoration of Austrey, Warwickshire, (1844–5: Fig. 8a) was 'the first foundation stone of success', that of Scarborough 'the corner stone of success' – a nice architectural distinction – and that of Wolverhampton (1852–65) 'a fruit' of Scarborough. But the memoir published shortly after Christian's death was in no doubt that it was his role as consulting architect of the Lichfield Diocesan Church Building Society, 'his first unsolicited honour', that 'gained for him' the Ecclesiastical Commission job.[27] The bishop of Lichfield at the time – John Lonsdale (bishop 1843–68) – was a friend of Christian and a hugely energetic church builder in his diocese, consecrating 156 new churches, many of which he helped fund with personal money drawn from his Sunk Island estate in the East Riding of Yorkshire. The building of the church there was entrusted to Christian (Fig. 9). The Commission role brought Christian a huge amount of business: Atkins counted 880 chancel restorations undertaken specifically for the Commission

Figs. 9a & b: Christian developed an effective formula for smaller churches – compact, simply detailed, with impressive apsidal east ends.
a: (top) Viney Hill, All Saints, Gloucestershire, 1865–7 (Author)
b: (bottom) Sunk Island, Holy Trinity, East Yorkshire, 1876–7.
(Colin Hinson)

and, on Christian's own reckoning, he carried out 'surveys and reports in detail on plans of churches, parsonage houses and other buildings averaging about 218 per annum'.[28]

It was the post of Ecclesiastical Commission architect that made Christian so widely known in his day. But it also rendered him vulnerable. His judgements on proposals that came before him were often severe and, as we have seen, caused resentment amongst some fellow-professionals who 'thought him exacting and capricious'.[29] G. G. Scott junior was rumoured to have shown his contempt of him by urinating on Christian's Hampstead doorstep.[30] Those churchmen, and there were many of them, who saw the Commission as a state agent bent on squeezing church funds, undermining its moral authority, and injecting a dose of Utilitarianism into its management, were not predisposed to welcome the interference of its architect (although no-one appears to have used the fact that Christian was married to a kinswoman of Jeremy Bentham – the founder of modern Utilitarianism – against him). This lay behind the rancour between the Dean and Chapter of Carlisle over Christian's restoration there, although this was as much directed against the reforming Dean Tait as Christian himself. Christian was not the chapter's choice but had been 'imposed on them' by the Commission; his limitations 'had become apparent' and they wished to turn to the more glamorous G. E. Street.[31] A similar, although less bitter, episode occurred at Southwell.[32]

The Liverpool Cathedral competition and the RIBA Royal Gold Medal

By the mid-1880s, the High Church party sensed its moment had arrived. The growing hostility to Christian and all he was seen to stand for came to a head over the first competition for Liverpool Cathedral (1884–8), for which Christian was appointed assessor, and Christian's candidacy for the RIBA Gold Medal in 1887. Liverpool was one of the three major cathedral projects on the British mainland during the last quarter of the nineteenth century, the others being St Mary's, Edinburgh, from 1874 (for which Christian had been the assessor) and Truro, from 1878–80, both still under construction at the time of the Liverpool affair.[33] Many thought a cathedral to be the logical next step after the creation of the new see of Liverpool in 1880. Others objected that such a project was superfluous to the needs of a city that was poorly provided with Anglican church places. This, it was argued, rendered it ill equipped to meet the needs of a rapidly growing working-class population or counter the perceived threat of Roman Catholicism. There were practical dilemmas, too, concerning the constricted nature of the proposed site adjoining St George's Hall and the whole project was plagued with serious budgetary uncertainties. These local problems, however, were in large measure reflections of deeper issues that polarised opinion and poisoned debate. The question of style was uppermost in people's minds. What was most appropriate for a modern, thriving, commercial, world city? The use of Gothic was the main bone of contention, as it had been at Truro – 'simply a medieval cathedral all over again' – and was to be later in the more famous Liverpool Cathedral competition of 1901–3. *The Builder* favoured a centralised 'peoples'' cathedral 'à la Wren', rather than 'a mere mediaeval imitation, which, in such a town as Liverpool, we should regard as little better than a costly anachronism'.[34] *The Architect* was equally hostile to the idea of a 'sham … in the gothic revival fashion [that] has gone out'. 'Liverpool is intensely modern, immensely wealthy, entirely commercial' and, stooping to sarcasm gleefully quoted in the *Liverpool Mercury*, it feared that the end result would have all the apparatus of a medieval monastery, including a 'sacristy and almonry; refectory, buttery, and dormitory, if not for the clergy, for the white-robbed [sic] choristers.'[35]

Questions of style were largely reflections of more profound tensions that had, by the middle years of the nineteenth century, created largely irresolvable strains between the Evangelicals and those with High Church and Anglo-Catholic sympathies. Competing interpretations of liturgy and doctrine necessarily impacted on architectural design. The debates intensified during the last two decades of the century as the influence of the Anglo-Catholic movement grew, not least over issues such as the provision and character of new cathedrals. Contemporary observers were quick to see the political drivers behind the debate over Liverpool. After the competition was shelved in 1888, ostensibly on financial grounds, *The Builder* opined that it had been 'the want of uniformity in the church itself [that] was the cause of the failure; the High Church party would not have a Low Church cathedral, and vice versa.'[36]

It was into this minefield of local and national disputes and animosities that Christian strode forth as assessor, with his usual diligence and fair-mindedness, but also (as we have seen) with the substantial baggage acquired as the evangelically orientated architect for the Ecclesiastical Commission. The experience gained in the latter post equipped him well for the Liverpool task and he was among the most frequently appointed competition judges in the British Isles. 101 portfolios were submitted to the competition sub-committee, chaired by Bishop Ryle of Liverpool. Twelve candidates were selected and, from these, four practices – Pearson (who later withdrew on grounds of overwork and ill-health), Bodley & Garner, Emerson, and Brooks – were invited to proceed to the second stage (August 1884). The process was very long winded, not least because it was necessary to steer a bill through parliament.[37] The short-listed designs were widely published in the national specialist press and exhibited at the Walker Art Gallery in Liverpool in January 1886, a show that attracted nearly 40,000 visitors.[38] In February 1886, Christian was formally invited to make a final decision. The *Building News* reported that it had heard from 'some usually well-informed quarters' that Christian was to be assisted by Pearson and E. G. Paley, but he professed to know of no such arrangement and would 'not shirk the responsibility of acting alone'.[39] In fact, Christian was struggling: he was working on the competition assessment one day a week as well as in his spare time and by the autumn he had fallen ill and needed to escape to Switzerland to recuperate.[40] His report was finally received in December.

Christian saw merits in all the entries but marginally favoured Emerson's. His decision was attacked on two related fronts: his High Church critics overtly attacked his credentials and ridiculed Emerson's designs; closer to home, Anglo-Catholic sympathisers and others within the architectural profession attacked the competition procedure and, by implication, also targeted Christian's *bona fides*.

Emerson's proposal was for a compressed plan in an early Gothic continental style with a dome at the crossing. He attempted to reconcile the competing pressures: a centralised plan, but in a Gothic style that was not redolent of Barchester, and which massed 'pyramidally' in order fully to exploit the inadequate site. Furthermore, it was technically innovative to suit a progressive city, being fully fireproofed with a concrete roof structure. The *Church Times*, already angry with the bishop of Liverpool, an eminent Evangelical forcefully opposed to ritualism, and the object of High Church criticism, pulled no punches. On Christian:

> Three sets of plans have been sent in, and they are shortly to be reported on by the Ecclesiastical Commissioners' architect. Why this gentleman should be chosen as an arbiter is hard to understand. He has built no great church, and the works which he will hand down to posterity are a few minor parish churches, and a host of uninteresting parsonages.

And on Christian's choice:

> It exhibits a desire for originality, which, in these days, seems to go down so much more readily than cultivated appreciation of old forms. Mr Emerson's design would make an admirable Hall of Varieties, if it ceased to be used in the future for religious use. A subsidiary Winter Garden might be added to it without any violent severing of the

unities. An illuminated fountain rising from the dome area would be most effective, and an orchestral organ might be erected in the central apse. The building is fireproof, and the design shows knowledge of construction. Whether the immunity from danger thus ensured would be a gain we must leave posterity to determine.[41]

A new front was opened early in 1887 when 'a considerable hubbub' broke out at the RIBA regarding the competition and Christian's role as assessor. In February, John Oldrid Scott and J. P. Seddon – the former an Anglo-Catholic, the latter of Evangelical persuasion but one who appears never to have got on with Christian[42] – circulated a petition demanding that the exhibition of the competition drawings shown at Liverpool be transferred to London 'for the purpose of eliciting the best skilled and widest public opinion of them': in other words re-opening the issue. There were two principles at stake: one (despite the involvement of Seddon) was the impropriety of using a professional issue as a stalking horse for the High-Church party; the other was the danger that the petition posed to the hard-won battle to secure professional assessors in public architectural competitions. On the former, *The Builder* was in no doubt 'that the "most skilled public opinion" really means the "church party" who want to stereotype church architecture on the medieval model' and 'attempt to set aside Mr Christian's very able report'. [43] *The Building News* was sufficiently incensed to threaten Scott and Seddon with publishing information that the two gentlemen would find 'not altogether palatable'.[44] Christian himself, however, did not impute sinister motives on the part of the petitioners and indicated that he had no objection to a London show provided that his report accompanied it.[45]

It was left to other RIBA activists, who appreciated the wider threat to the profession, to join battle. A reformed system whereby competition organisers appoint professional assessors nominated by the Institute's president was still bedding in.[46] Scandals surrounding individual cases could bring the whole system into ill-repute, a point not lost on the *Building News*, which saw the acrimonious criticisms following Christian's award such as to drive 'a coach and horses through the recently-won procedure of moving forward by competition and accepting judgement by professional assessors'. [47] The Institute council made every effort to distance itself from the petition, recognising (as one member put it) 'that it would be little short of a calamity if the action taken [by Scott and Seddon was] allowed to obtain without some decided protest from the [RIBA]' and (according to another) that it 'would throw a most undeserved slur upon one whom this institute has always trusted and delighted to honour [and] bring the profession into disrepute'. [48] While the wording of the petition was amended, Scott still circulated it and implied that it had the approval of the Institute – an act of omission that he later accepted was 'an error of judgement' on his part. [49] But the damage was done: the petition attracted many signatories (most 'unknown to fame' sneered *The Builder*). Many of them were mortified when they realised how their support had been manipulated in the attack on Christian. [50]

The whole business of the challenge to the competition result was bound up with Christian's nomination for the RIBA Royal Gold Medal – a connection that did not escape the Liverpool papers, which leaked the fact that the Gold Medal decision was not unanimous as part of their coverage of the Scott and Seddon petition. Innuendos were abroad about other competition judgements made by Christian – including the Admiralty building and a number of London churches – and the RIBA council was clearly alarmed at the damage a bodged Gold Medal nomination would cause to its credibility, especially following the embarrassment over the award to Butterfield a few years before when he declined to accept it personally. The smart money was on Richard Norman Shaw, but he had no time for the RIBA and indicated to Aston Webb that he would not 'look at the Gold Medal [being] strongly opposed to the whole thing'. [51] Given that Shaw's 'great artistic talent place[d] him foremost', his refusal to consider receiving the medal left the other candidates 'so much on a par' that William Fawcett, for one, recommended turning to an American in order 'not to provoke insidious comparison'. [52] In the event, Christian received his medal (in May) but there was little room to doubt that the whole shoddy episode revealed the clash of two architectural cultures: those (such as Scott, Seddon and Shaw) who saw their profession as a form of high art and who disdained the RIBA, which they saw 'as a mere trade union', [53] and the institute reformers and committee men, such as Christian, whom by implication they dismissed as mechanical hacks.

By the time of his death, these negative views had become well established. 'Always in excellent taste … he became over fastidious, and designed as if his powers were restricted' opined *The Builder* in its obituary, a view echoed by *Building News:* 'in no sense a heaven-born genius, or even possessed of brilliant parts, but a man of inflexible honesty, great industry, and good business capabilities, he was a safe pair of hands'. [54] It is not possible to weigh with any precision the relative importance of all the factors at play in the formation of Christian's reputation – the entrenched positions outlined in the preceding paragraphs; the role of economy in so much of his work, especially when carried out for the Ecclesiastical Commission; and his concern above all for sound construction and fitness for use. But there is, in addition, a conscious aesthetic that favoured simplicity. Christian himself realised that this tendency would not always commend itself to clients or to the tastes of the day. He admired the tower of S. Zeno in Verona, which rises 200 feet without ornament: of its effect, he wrote: 'I can fancy what a fuss would be made in our country … people would say, "how bare and ugly it is!" and yet these great architects knew what they were about, and everybody allows that the result is beautiful. They look so grand and dignified. I delight in them.'[55]

Notes

1   This paper does not narrate Christian's life and career in detail. These are set out in the *Oxford Dictionary of National Biography* via http://www. oxforddnb.com/view/article/62459 but the fullest coverage is Anon., *Ewan Christian, Architect* (Cambridge, 1896), hereafter *Christian* – a collection of essays, probably edited by Elizabeth Rundle Charles. Also J. Standen Adkins, 'Ewan Christian: A Memoir', *Journal of the Royal Institute of British Architects*, 3rd ser., 18 (1911), 711–30, contains a selective list of works derived largely from one drawn up in part by Christian himself, a photocopy of which is kept in the Royal Institute of British Architects library (biographical file for Christian). It is hereafter referred to as 'RIBA list of works'. Some of this published material is usefully summarised in Ann Stocker, 'The Life and Work of Ewan Christian' (unpublished Architectural Association conservation course thesis, 1981). Although he designed many secular buildings, most famously the National Portrait Gallery, he is best known as a church architect and it is this side of his output that is discussed here.

2   Basil F. L. Clarke, *Church Builders of the Nineteenth Century: A Study of the Gothic Revival in England* (1938, reprinted Newton Abbot, 1969). This is an inference drawn from a number of dismissive comments Clarke made about both architects, but especially (p. 192) where they are singled out as exemplifying lack of character: the buildings of Scott 'above all, and those of others, such as Ewan Christian'.

3   Nikolaus Pevsner, *The Buildings of England: Nottinghamshire* (Harmondsworth, 1951), 156, and repeated in the 2nd ed. (rev. Elizabeth Williamson, Harmondsworth, 1979), 308.

4   Ian Nairn & Nikolaus Pevsner, *The Buildings of England: Sussex* (Harmondsworth, 1965), 77.

5   Clarke, *Church Builders*, 159.

6   J. Mordaunt Crook, *William Burges and the Victorian Dream* (London, 1981), 80; A. Quiney, *John Loughborough Pearson* (New Haven & London, 1979), 84.

7   Nikolaus Pevsner, *The Buildings of England: London II* (Harmondsworth, 1952), 429. Bridget Cherry tactfully removed the phrase in her revised edition: *London 4: North* (Harmondsworth, 1998, corrected 1999), 537.

8   Stefan Muthesius, *The High Victorian Movement in Architecture 1850–1870* (London, 1972), 53.

9   Peter F. Anson, *Fashions in Church Furnishings 1840–1940* (London, 1960), 122, 241–2.

10 Charles E. Eastlake, *A History of the Gothic Revival* (Leicester, 1978), 210. Originally published in 1872, this reprint is edited with much new information by J. Mordaunt Crook.

11 Eastlake, *Gothic Revival*, 289.

12 George H. Birch, 'Work' (chapter II) in *Christian*, 61. This is a corrected and enlarged version of his memoir in *Journal RIBA*, 3rd ser., 2 (1895), 331–4.

13 *The Ecclesiologist*, 8 (1848), 123.

14 Ibid., 14 (1853), 455.

15 John Newman, *The Buildings of England: West Kent and the Weald* (Harmondsworth, 1969), 109, 317.

16 Julian Orbach, *Victorian Architecture in Britain* (London, 1987), 127.

17 As described by Christian himself when accepting the RIBA Gold Medal.

18 Matthew Habershon, *The Ancient Half-Timbered Houses of England* (London, 1836), preface.

19 *Christian*, 54.

20 Ewan Christian, *Architectural Illustrations of Skelton Church Yorkshire* (London, 1846).

21 *Christian*, 22–3.

22 Paul Thompson, *William Butterfield* (London & Cambridge, Mass., 1971), 167.

23 *J Procs RIBA*, n.s. 3 (1887), 305.

24 Harold Brooke, *Closed for Business: Ewan Christian's Restoration of Southwell Minster 1848–1888* (Southwell Minster Cathedral Council, 1997), 53.

25 *J Procs RIBA*, n.s. 2 (1886), 186.

26 See note 1. The RIBA list of works is the source of the quotations that follow, which are in Christian's hand, although the document itself is of composite authorship. It was probably compiled in connection with his candidacy for the 1887 Gold Medal.

27 *Christian*, 20.

28 RIBA list of works. Adkins, *Memoir*, 726. Adkins breaks down Christian's work thus: 90 new churches, 400 church restorations, 880 chancel restorations for the Commission, 10 parochial and mission halls, 40 capitular and Episcopal residences, 380 clergy houses, 80 schools, 120 private residences, 20 commercial buildings and 20 others (that included the National Portrait Gallery).

29 *Christian*, 60.

30 Gavin Stamp, *An Architect of Promise: George Gilbert Scott Junior (1839–1897) and the Late Gothic Revival* (Donington, 2002), 337 n.55.

31 Graeme Knowles, 'Archbishop Campbell Tait, Dean of Carlisle 1850 to 1856, and Ewan Christian, Architect' in Mike McCathy and David Weston (eds.), *Carlisle and Cumbria: Roman and Medieval Art and Archaeology* (BAA conference transactions, 27 Leeds, 2004), 233–4.

32 Brooke, *Closed for Business, 32*.

33 Christian's role in the Edinburgh competition is usefully analysed by Alistair Rowan, 'Penetrating the incognito: St Mary's Cathedral, Edinburgh' in Frank Salmon (ed.), *Gothic and the Gothic Revival* (papers of the 26th symposium of the Society of Architectural Historians of Great Britain, 1997: Manchester, 1998), 99–114.

34 *The Builder*, 47 (1884), 516.

35 *The Architect*, 31 (1884), 127; *Liverpool Mercury*, 30 August 1884.

36 *The Builder*, 54 (1888), 278.

37 Ibid., 47 (1884), 51, 300, 848.

38 *Liverpool Mercury*, 10 February 1886; *The Builder*, 50 (1886), 225. The competition is discussed in Joan Bassin, *Architectural Competitions in Nineteenth-century England* (Ann Arbor, Michigan/UMI Research Press, 1984), chapter 6.

39 *Building News*, 50 (1886), 255, 296.

40 Ibid., 51 (1886), 147, 405.

41 *Church Times*, 18 June 1886, 478–9.

42 I am indebted to Tye Blackshaw for advice on the relationship between Seddon and Christian.

43 *The Builder*, 52 (1887), 209, 249.

44 *Building News*, 52 (1887), 233.

45 *The Architect*, 37 (1887), 156.

46 Roger H. Harper, *Victorian Architectural Competitions* (London, 1983), xxiii–iv, 201.

47 *Building News*, 51 (1886), 155.

48 RIBA British Architectural Library and Archive LC/25/7/14i (letters from G. A. Audesley and Cole Adams)

49 *J Procs RIBA*, n.s. 3 (1887), 199.

50 Much of the subsequent correspondence expressing outrage is summarised in *Building News*, 52 (1887), 217, 261, 299, 239, 457.

51 *J Procs RIBA*, n.s. 3 (1887), 199.

52 Ibid., LC/25/7/4.

53 This refers to Shaw: *Oxford Dictionary of National Biography* via http://www.oxforddnb/36050 (Andrew Saint).

54 *The Builder*, 68 (1895), 170; *Building News*, 68 (1895), 320–1.

55 Letter from Christian quoted in Standen Adkins, 'Ewan Christian' (*see* note 1), 728.

'Inventive and ingenious': designs by William White

Gill Hunter

IT IS UNSURPRISING that an architect who in 1871 patented his design for a frame rucksack – an idea not resuscitated until the latter half of the twentieth century – should have been described, in one of his obituaries, as possessing a talent that was 'inventive and ingenious'.[1] As a scion of a clerical family that also embraced scientific principles (Gilbert White of Selborne, the great naturalist, was his great-uncle), William White inherited a deep love and interest in the natural world and a belief in the ability of technology to improve living and working conditions. He recognised the benefits of double-glazing, and the employment of dormer windows in churches where a clerestory would be too costly; and he appears to have invented a modern system of herringbone wood-block flooring, and the decorative over-painting of brickwork. White's scientific interest in human anatomy was reflected in his proposals for comfortable church seating. Although he refused to admit iron as a legitimate building material, White was prepared to experiment with concrete. At St Peter's, Linkenholt in Hampshire (1869–71), and the adjacent school (1871), he used local fossils, known as 'Shepherds' Crowns', to decorate the heads of some of the windows.[2] White's interest in ironwork manifested itself not only in traditional church fittings, such as candelabra and reading desks, but in creative designs for catches and gates.

Double-glazing

In 1847 after only two years as an 'improver' in George Gilbert Scott's office, White had left London to establish his own practice in Truro, Cornwall. He returned to the capital in 1851–2 in connection with his first London commission, All Saints', Notting Hill. Intended as a collegiate church with attached choir school, it was designed for the Revd Dr Samuel Edmund Walker, the incumbent of St Columb Major, Cornwall, in memory of his parents. Described by *The Ecclesiologist* as 'of great size and dignity', it was unfinished when Dr Walker's investments in speculative property developments failed in 1854.[3] It was finally consecrated in 1861, having been completed (apart from White's planned spire and western flying buttresses) under the superintendence of a civil engineer. *The Ecclesiologist* noted 'the strange openings, and the feeble reredos of sham materials'.[4] White was provoked to request that 'it should be stated that it was put into the hands of a civil engineer, lest any reflection should be cast upon the architectural profession'![5] Unfortunately the church was badly damaged by bombs in World War II, including the destruction of all the glass. There is no remaining evidence,

Gill Hunter was awarded a PhD in 2007 for her research on William White. Her monograph on the architect will be published later this year.

therefore, of the double-glazing that White later said he had employed at All Saints' in order to keep out 'cold and noise'. He reported that the results were 'highly satisfactory', and advised that 'it might be adopted with advantage more often than it is at present'.[6]

White's use of double-glazing can still be seen in the west window of the church of St John the Baptist, Leusdon, near Widecombe-in-the-Moor in Devon. An elder brother, the Revd Francis Gilbert White, was incumbent there when the founder of the church, Mrs Charlotte Rosamond Larpent, died in April 1879. 'Upwards of a hundred of her friends and fellow parishioners' subscribed 'sums varying from twopence to ten pounds' for a stained glass window in her memory.[7] *Church Bells* reported that this 'most successful stained-glass window' depicting four scenes from the life of the Baptist, surrounded by geometric patterning, was 'designed and executed by Mr William White' (Fig. 1) for a little over £120.[8] The plain glass set in the exterior of the new tracery ensured not only warmth, but protection for the stained work and its leading from the intense wind and rain experienced at the church's exposed hill-top position.

Wood-block flooring

There is further evidence of White's belief in improving comfort in churches. On 10 February 1857 he asked for the sanction of the Incorporated Church Building Society (ICBS) to an alteration in the specification for his restoration of St Mildred's church at Preston by Wingham, Kent. His request was to replace the boarded floor and joists under the seats with 'wood blocks 9 x 4½ x 1½ ins thick laid herring bone fashion in lime and hair upon a properly prepared bed.'[9] There was no objection to White's proposal, but it was followed on 12 March by a sketch showing that blocks, 13½ ins by 4½ ins by 1½ ins, were to be laid in a herringbone pattern on 4 ins of concrete.[10] In 1890 White claimed that 'not far from 40 years ago' he had 'first invented the flat wood-block paving'.[11] White's niece, daughter of the Revd Henry Master White, later reported that William refused to take out a patent on this system of flooring that was 'strong … pleasant to the foot and comparatively noiseless, for he said that it was far too useful for anyone to be debarred from using it'.[12] It can be seen in many of his designs for houses, as well as for new and restored churches, such as St Peter, Mithian, Cornwall (1850–61), St Michael & All Angels, Lyndhurst, Hampshire (1858–69), All Saints, Newland, Gloucestershire (1861–2), St Mary, Longstock, Hampshire (1876–80), St Michael, Battersea (1880–3) and St Peter, Little Comberton, Worcestershire (1885–6).

Fig. 1: Leusdon, St John, Devon, west window designed and executed by William White, 1879. (Author)

White was not alone in his use of wood blocks. Originally in May 1855 G. E. Street specified deal boards on joists for the floor in his restoration of St Mary the Virgin, Upton Scudamore in Wiltshire.[13] But by October, it had been agreed that for an extra sum of £90 16s 10d the contractor should lay wood-block paving on a concrete bed.[14] These are heartwood blocks approximately 6¾ x 5½ x 1¾ ins, laid in courses like bricks. Although there is a herringbone patterned wood-block floor in the church at Bierton, restored by Street 1852–3, this was not laid until 1926.[15] When G. F. Bodley used wood-block flooring at St John, Tue Brook, Liverpool, in 1871, it was noted that 'The floors are formed of blocks of oak – a novelty and a luxury which will be greatly appreciated in cold weather'.[16]

Seating

Church seating was, and still is, a topic of concern to all parishioners. White's condemnation of tight clothing and high-heeled shoes and his adoption, with all his family, of a system of Swedish gymnastics, demonstrate his concern with correct posture and physical fitness. He wrote a paper, 'Church Seats', published by the *Church Builder* for 1884, in which he pointed out that sloping backs to seats were 'pre-eminently uncomfortable … except to those whose backs have become bent to the required extent'.[17] White believed that everyone 'should be taught from their earliest childhood to sit well back in the seat of a properly formed chair'.[18] However, a high or sloping back to a seat would prevent this (Fig. 2, see White's Fig. C). White's solution (White's Fig. B) was designed to support the back of the occupant. He pointed out that his design was not 'in strict accord with the rigid architectural lines of the medieval benches' reproduced in many churches (White's Fig. A), but admitted 'there are not very many in these days who will patiently and implicitly take on faith that it must be the proper thing'. White wrote to William H. White, Secretary of the R.I.B.A., enclosing a copy of his paper, which he remarked waspishly, 'I would specially commend to your notice in case of any future alteration in the seats of the Lecture Hall, which at present contribute to anything but the mental repose so needful for the ready reception of scientific information, or the relief of the backs of those who may be supposed to have done a hard day's work'.[19]

Dormer windows

At St Mildred's, Preston, can be seen the large triangular dormers that White used where light was required but a clerestory was inappropriate or too costly (Fig. 3). Although *The Ecclesiologist* reported that White's restoration (1855–8) included the blocking

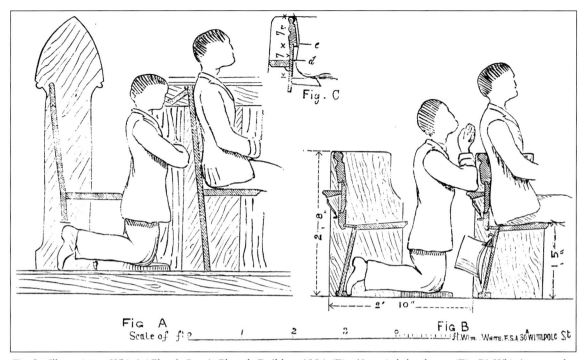

Fig. 2: Illustration to White's 'Church Seats', Church Builder, *1884. 'Fig. A', typical church seat; 'Fig. B', White's proposed design; 'Fig. C', showing how poor design prevents correct posture and proper support.*

of the 'small, and mutilated, and inconvenient' windows of the aisles, a watercolour of 1807 shows that this had been done earlier, and that three small conventional dormers had previously been inserted on the north side.[20] White's two triangular dormers on each side of the nave were described by *The Ecclesiologist* as 'extremely picturesque externally, and internally the light is abundant and very agreeably diffused – as if from a clerestory'.[21] The Ecclesiological Society admitted 'a special interest' in this restoration, for the incumbent, the Revd Henry Lascelles Jenner, was a committee member and the Secretary for Music.[22] *The Ecclesiologist* lavishly praised the 'simplicity and reality' of the work, resulting in a 'real restoration, and not a needless obliteration of ancient features. … we have seldom seen a better'.

At the same time that White was engaged at Preston, George Gilbert Scott was designing the dining hall at Bradfield College in Berkshire, for the Revd Thomas Stevens. Scott's design also featured large triangular dormers. Did one man influence the other, or did both find the same solution to the problem at roughly the same time? Curiously, Hampshire Record Office holds what purports to be the transcript of a letter from G. G. Scott to William White concerning White's design for the parish church at Lyndhurst. Answering 'the questions put to me respecting your design', Scott admitted that a clerestory would render the church too tall for its length, and would require more

Fig. 3: Preston by Wingham,
St Mildred, Kent, showing the
previously blocked aisle windows and
White's dormers of 1855–7. (Author)

Fig. 4: Lyndhurst, St Michael and All Angels, Hampshire,
one of two triangular dormers to north side of the nave.
(Author)

substantial arcades.[23] Scott concluded that 'I am decidedly favourable to the idea of Gabled lights … they will I am sure look well both within and without and will give the church an individuality of character which it is not always easy to obtain'. In the event, *The Ecclesiologist* did not approve of White's dormers at Lyndhurst (Fig. 4), criticising particularly the 'host of geometrical figures, very crudely combined, in the heads'.[24]

Concrete construction

In 1858 the incumbent of Lyndhurst, the Revd John Compton, had applied to the Incorporated Church Building Society for a grant towards the cost of re-building his church of St Michael and All Angels to White's design. White proposed that all walls with a thickness greater than two and a half bricks were to have their centres filled with concrete; the ICBS insisted that alternate courses should be bonded.[25] There is no further mention of this method of construction at Lyndhurst, so it may well have been abandoned along with White's first set of plans.

It re-appears in 1873 when White was designing St Mark's, Battersea Rise in south London, for the Revd John Erskine Clarke (Fig. 5). Here White specified concrete within exterior and interior casings of 4½in brickwork, bonding being provided by a

Fig. 5: Battersea Rise, St Mark, built to White's 1873 design in brick and concrete. (Geoff Brandwood)

complete course of bricks every tenth course, and a course of headers projecting into the walls every intermediate fifth course.[26] White had to submit a sample of his method of construction in order to obtain permission for its use from the Metropolitan Board of Works and from the district surveyor. The licence stipulated that cement mortar, rather than common lime mortar, was to be used for the brick casing, which added £112 to the cost.

G. E. Street, as diocesan architect (Battersea being at that time in the diocese of Winchester) believed that a clerk of works should be employed to supervise the construction, and that the bonding should be of three courses. White defended his method, pointing out that Roman walls of similar construction, but with no bonding courses, were still standing. Representatives of the ICBS Committee of Architects visited the site to inspect White's method of construction before agreeing to the provision of a grant of £300, although they pointed out that this 'ought not to be considered as a precedent of their approval of the use of brick and concrete together'.[27] The walls could only be raised up by about two feet a day to allow the concrete to set, so a longer stretch of wall needed to be scaffolded. Although the concrete was cheaper than the equivalent volume of bricks, White realised that the increased labour costs made this method uneconomical and did not use it again.[28]

Forest School, Walthamstow

In December 1855 the philanthropist, William Cotton, a founder and trustee of Forest School, Walthamstow, had initiated the building of a chapel at the school as a tribute to the headmaster, Dr John Gilderdale.[29] Other subscribers included the Hon. Mr Justice Coleridge, Philip Cazenove and a Miss Morris, probably an aunt or sister of William Morris. *The Ecclesiologist* reported that three choral exhibitions of 30 guineas each had been endowed at the school, 'where also a chapel is being erected, with due choral arrangements, from designs by our member, Mr. White'.[30] On 11 June 1857, William's brother, the Revd Francis Gilbert White married John Gilderdale's daughter, Lucy. Her elder sister, Rebecca, had married the Revd Frederick Barlow Guy, a former pupil of her father, in 1852. Guy returned to teach at the school in 1857, taking over from Dr Gilderdale about the time of the opening of the chapel on 24 June in that year.[31] Apparently Frederick Guy and William White shared an interest in walking in the Lake District, and White attended Speech Days 'and watched the progress of the school with keen interest'.[32] In 1875 Guy commissioned William White to design an enlargement of the chancel of the school chapel. The work was completed by 1878 (including a wood-block floor), and at the same time four triangular dormers were inserted, one on each side of the nave and chancel (Fig. 6). Perhaps more light was required as a western gallery was inserted, and the original windows were gradually filled with stained glass.

Mural decoration

Although the chapel at Forest School is constructed of polychrome brick, there is no surviving evidence that it was ever decorated internally with White's system of over-painting. White's magnificent brick church of St Saviour, Aberdeen Park in Islington, appears to be the first building where he employed this lace-like stencilling. The church was designed in 1863 for and built at the sole cost of, White's brother-in-law, the Revd William David Morrice, vicar of Longbridge Deverill, Wiltshire, and a founder member of the Cambridge Camden Society, on land he had inherited.[33] Inspired by the Oxford Movement, Morrice wanted to provide High Church services, including daily prayers and communion twice each Sunday, to an area served by the Evangelical Christ Church in Highbury Grove.

Fig. 6: North elevation of the chapel, Forest School, Walthamstow, designed by White in 1856, (turret and spire, by White, added 1866–9), extended westwards and dormers inserted 1875–8. (Author)

The extravagant height of White's small cruciform church with its squat central tower and octagonal spire is emphasised by the patterning of the brickwork in the upper walls and gable ends. Inside the chancel the red brickwork, with patterns of buff and black bricks, was decorated with a design of chevrons, stylised flowers and leaves set in circles, diamonds and triangles, all thinly painted to give an effect of lace (Fig. 7). It allowed an integration of the structural polychromy with motifs in the stained glass and the encaustic floor tiles. A report of the roughness of the internal brickwork was pardoned in the knowledge that the intention was to have 'the whole of the walls diapered in colour, with the brickwork for a ground', in the same manner as had been completed on the east wall.[34] Remarking on this painting, 'executed by Mr. H. Davies, from designs by William White, Esq.', *The Guardian* noted 'how much may be done with merely a ground of common brick when picked out in colour.'[35] Henry Davies had assisted Thomas Gambier Parry with the painting of the ceiling of Ely Cathedral. He went on to execute White's mural and ceiling designs and painted furniture at Quy Hall, Cambridge, and at Humewood Castle, Co. Wicklow.

Fig. 7: Islington, St Saviour, Aberdeen Park, 1863–9, (now Florence Trust Artists' Studios), painted decoration to chancel. (Author)

White's system of painting over brickwork can also be seen at the church of St Philip and St James, Maryfield in Cornwall (1864–71), and at St Petrock's, Farringdon, Devon (1870–1). In 1893 he was commissioned to extend the tiny Christ Church, Smannell, Hampshire, that he had designed in 1856–7, by widening the original lean-to north aisle and gabling it, adding a choir vestry and space for an organ. The incumbent of Smannell reported to the Diocesan Registry that 'Decoration of the East End, under the direction of W. White, Esq., Architect, forms part of our work'.[36] White's design for stencilling over the polychromatic brickwork of the chancel included conventionalised plant forms like espaliered fruit trees, similar to some of his ironwork (Fig. 8). The window reveals are decorated with simpler plant 'stems' and diamonds containing angels and crosses. This fairly simple form of decoration celebrates the materials and structure of the building. It is a relatively cheap form

Fig. 8: Christ Church, Smannell, Hampshire, painted decoration in the chancel, 1893–4. (Author)

of adornment that could be applied by local craftsmen, making it ideal for a small country church that originally cost less than £700 to build.

Ironwork

In 1858 White was commissioned to restore the church of St Michael at Bradden, Northamptonshire. The incumbent was the Revd Cornelius Ives, a cousin of White's mother.[37] Although mentioned in *The Ecclesiologist* as being repaired, with a new nave roof, White's scheme was a virtual rebuilding, only the thirteenth-century tower and arcades surviving.[38] Included in a list of the expenses is £2 4s. for an iron gate.[39] The ironwork of this entrance on the southern boundary of the churchyard has survived (Fig. 9). It is a simple and ingenious latch operated by downward pressure on the elegantly curved bar, making it easy to use for those with arthritic fingers, or people carrying tools, flowers, etc. to the church. A similar latch, but with an unadorned top bar, can be seen on the paddock gate at White's magnificent vicarage for the Revd Robert Calthrop at Irton, near Seascale in Cumbria (1864–6).

The Revd John Erskine Clarke, rector of Battersea, was also patron of the parish of Elvington, near York. Here in the early years of the nineteenth century the medieval church of the Holy Trinity had been rebuilt by his maternal ancestor, the Revd Cheap. In 1865 Clarke's younger brother, the Revd Alured Clarke was appointed to the living of Elvington. By 1874 Alured Clarke determined to rebuild the church on a site within the churchyard, but further to the south.[40] However, the contract for the construction, to William White's plans and specification, by J. Keswick & Sons of York, was not signed until 26 April 1876, with completion specified as 25 February the following year.[41] White devised a boundary fence of iron bars, their curved tips the only ornamentation, set diagonally on a brick plinth with stone-capped brick piers. A 'kissing gate' was constructed from two sections of ironwork, the swinging portion identified by crossing the diagonals to form a diamond pattern (Fig. 10). This simple and economical solution maintains an unbroken boundary with no interruption to the view of the church.

These are just a few examples of White's inventive solutions to problems that often arose because of constraints of cost. As he pointed out in a paper on 'Cheap Churches', 'an article may be cheap without being nasty, or nasty without being cheap'.[42] White warned of the danger of 'poverty decked out in tinsel or trumpery ornament [that] can only call attention to its own degradation'.[43] However, he believed that 'mural decoration is quite compatible with the greatest simplicity of construction'.[44] Cheap building was

Fig. 9: Bradden, St Michael, Northamptonshire, southerly entrance gate to churchyard with White's ingenious latch, 1858–9. (Author)

Fig: 10.Elvington, Holy Trinity, North Yorkshire, 1874–8, churchyard gate. (Author)

often, White believed, 'a necessary evil … But it is in one sense a school of art. It teaches us the best, the most natural, the most simple modes of construction, and fits us for the better use of our higher opportunities'.[45]

Notes

1 *Architectural Association Notes*, 15 (1900), 20.
2 Gill Hunter, 'Cheap & Cheerful: William White in Hampshire', *Ecclesiology Today*, 22 (2000), 31.
3 *The Ecclesiologist*, 13 (1852), 299.
4 Ibid. 22, (1861), 328.
5 Ibid., 246.
6 *Church Bells*, 24 March 1883, 310.
7 Ibid., 17 January 1880, 106.
8 Ibid.
9 ICBS file 5056, Lambeth Palace Library
10 Ibid. Can be seen on www.churchplansonline.org
11 *Building News*, 58 (1890), 224. I am very grateful to Geoff Brandwood for bringing this to my attention.
12 Miss H.M.White, *Cameos*, September 1960, Bishops College Archive, Cape Town.
13 Specification, Wiltshire Record Office, D1/61/8/19.
14 Addition A to specification, Wiltshire Record Office, PR/Upton Scudamore, St Mary the Virgin/1741/21.
15 Faculty, Oxfordshire Record Office MS Oxf.Dioc Papers, c.1346. I am very grateful to Paul Joyce for information concerning Street's restoration at Bierton, and at Hulcott, Buckinghamshire (1861–3).
16 'Consecration of the Church of St John the Baptist', supplement to the *Liverpool Daily Post*, 22 May 1871. I am very grateful to Michael Hall for bringing this to my attention.
17 *Church Builder* (1884) 108–15.
18 Ibid., 110.
19 RIBA Library, March 1885, WhW/Pam78, fols. 441–3.
20 *The Ecclesiologist*, 18 (1857), 323; H. Petrie, F.S.A., ref. 285, Kent Archaeological Society.
21 *The Ecclesiologist*, 18 (1857), 323.
22 Geoff Brandwood, 'A Camdenian Roll-Call', C. Webster & J. P. Elliott (eds.), *'A Church as it Should be'* (Stamford, 2000), 408.

23 Hampshire Record Office, 25M84/PW25, no date.
24 *The Ecclesiologist*, 17 (1859), 288.
25 ICBS file 5267, Lambeth Palace Library, application, 29 May 1858; White's letter, 11 June 1858.
26 William White, 'A Brick and Concrete Church', *The Builder*, 33 (1875), 48–50.
27 ICBS file 5267, resolution, 6 May 1874.
28 When White restored St Leonard's, Sandridge, Hertfordshire in 1886–7, the tower was built of concrete, faced with flints externally and bricks on the inside.
29 Guy Deaton, *Schola Sylvestris* (1984), 64–5. Cotton offered £100 if the remaining monies could be raised within twelve months.
30 *The Ecclesiologist*, 18 (1857), 10.
31 Deaton, 65.
32 Ibid., 69: *Forest School Magazine*, Lent 1900, 298. I am very grateful to Adrienne Reynolds for this reference.
33 Morrice's wife, Esther, and White's wife, Ellen, were daughters of the Revd George Cornish, rector of Kenwyn and Kea, friend and contemporary of John Keble, Thomas Arnold and John Coleridge at Oxford.
34 *The Builder*, 25 (1867), 550.
35 *The Guardian*, 17 March 1869, 295. I am very grateful to Michael Kerney for bringing this reference to my attention. The first incumbent, the Revd John Bicknell, stated in 1881 that part of the chancel decoration by Davies was 'not immediately under his [White's] direction'. Church of England Record Centre, Gordon Barnes' Collection, N. London Churches, ISL/3/3a.
36 Letter from the Revd Eimer Coles, 20 November 1893, together with White's drawing, undated, Hampshire Record Office, 21M65/336F/1.
37 Cornelius's mother was the sister of William Van Mildert, last Prince-Bishop of Durham.
38 *The Ecclesiologist*, 19 (1858), 198; builder's account 1859, Northamptonshire Record Office Grant-Ives Collection 433.
39 Ibid., 434.
40 White's perspective from the north-east, dated 15 December 1874, in the church; citation, 10 February 1876, University of York, Borthwick Institute, FAC 1876/4a.
41 Memorandum of agreement, University of York, Borthwick Institute, PR ELV 23.
42 *Church Builder* (1881), 70.
43 Ibid.
44 Ibid., 92.
45 Ibid., 99.

'An architect of many churches': John Pollard Seddon

Tye R. Blackshaw

Tye Blackshaw has a BA in art history from Wellesley College, Massachusetts, USA, and an MA in medieval art from the Courtauld Institute. She became interested in Seddon while working on The Buildings of England, London 4: North West *and completed her PhD at the Courtauld in 2001 on his life and work before 1885.*

ADDRESSING the Church Congress in 1872, the architect J. P. Seddon (1827–1906) paid tribute to the Established Church for its enduring encouragement of architecture. In his view, it had diligently preserved precious medieval buildings throughout three centuries of 'really dark ages', then taken the lead in the early 1800s 'in the good work of reviving our old national style'. Still more recently, ecclesiastical patronage had resisted the cynical, commercial tendencies of the day, and remained true to the pursuit of high artistic values.[1]

The bias of these comments is understandable, yet it should not be assumed that Seddon merely wished to please his audience. In fact, there probably was no bias, because, for him, it was simply a statement of truth. Having been seduced as a young man by John Ruskin's passion and romantic pedagogy, Seddon subsequently acquired his fierce loyalty to the Gothic Revival, a stylistic predilection which, as for many like-minded architects, then developed effortlessly into a career of church design.

Early biography and influences

Seddon was born in the City of London on 19 September 1827, a great-grandson of George Seddon, founder of the prestigious Georgian cabinet-makers, Seddon & Co.[2] What his parents intended for Seddon's future is not clear. The firm was still active during Seddon's childhood under the proprietorship of his father, but it was his brother Thomas (1821–56) who was expected to take over. In the event, Thomas could not reconcile himself to the furniture trade, preferring instead a career in the fine arts. Toward this end, he enrolled in T. L. Donaldson's newly formed architectural course at University College, London, in 1842. Professor and pupil soon became close friends and in 1847, Donaldson made a relatively rare offer of articles to Thomas's younger brother, John, then aged 20.[3]

Donaldson generally designed in a classical idiom, and Seddon's later tendency toward regular and symmetrical plans and bold geometric groupings probably owed a good deal to this early training experience. But Seddon was not inspired to show any allegiance to the details of classical architecture and was soon devoted to practising in a 'widely different field to that in which he had received his early education', namely the Gothic Revival.[4]

By the late 1840s Pugin and the Ecclesiologists had very successfully propelled this movement to the forefront of architectural practice and away from fringe antiquarianism. But

83

their churchmanship held no appeal for the young J. P. Seddon. Raised against a background of Evangelical social reform, he found their Catholic or Tractarian overtones unpalatable.[5] Indeed, Seddon would remain a resolutely Broad Churchman throughout his life, and was at times even open to Low Church philosophy when it came to designing functional church plans. Thus, it was John Ruskin who played the pivotal role in converting the young J. P. Seddon to the Gothic Revival, and publication of *The Seven Lamps of Architecture* in 1849 the critical event. The profound effect of this book on Seddon was immediately evident in both his writings and travels that followed in 1850–51.[6] (Figs. 1 & 2). Unencumbered by overt religious dogma but no less emotionally charged than Puginian arguments, Ruskin's powerful reasoning and evocative eulogies of Gothic architecture were what ultimately awakened Seddon's own belief in its validity over all other styles.

Fig. 1: Plate VI from Progress in Art and Architecture with Precedents for Ornament, *1852. Details from Early French Gothic architecture in Normandy which Seddon drew during his trip there in the autumn of 1850. Of particular note are the stylistic similarities to plates in Ruskin's* The Seven Lamps of Architecture.

Thus set firmly on a Gothic path, Seddon commenced his architectural practice in London in the autumn of 1851.[7] There were a handful of small domestic commissions – boundary walls and town houses in London, and a cottage in Berkshire – although his handling of the Gothic style at this point was amateur and somewhat pedestrian. Then, late in 1852, Seddon began to apply inspiration from specifically local medieval precedents to his design for a small hotel on his uncle's seaside estate at Southerndown in Glamorgan. Eager to expand his repertoire further, he subsequently embarked on several tours of the vicinity, and in March 1853, on a visit to Llandaff Cathedral, he met the diocesan architect, John Prichard (1817–86), by whom he 'was most graciously received, and shewn all there was to be seen'. Clearly quite impressed with Seddon, Prichard offered him a partnership immediately thereafter.[8]

Hence, it was then under Prichard's competent guidance that Seddon's practical skills as an architect were honed and perfected from 1853. Prichard's professional position afforded him extensive access to all manner of ecclesiastical design, from cathedral to parish church, restoration to new build, fittings and fixtures to seat rearrangements. His scrupulous attention to stonework and sculptural detail synchronised perfectly with Seddon's Ruskinian aspirations. Furthermore, Prichard's demanding obligations to the Llandaff Cathedral fabric meant that Seddon soon found himself almost solely responsible, as he put it, for 'the smaller and more numerous [tasks] ... particularly those in Monmouthshire'.[9] These were primarily restorations or refittings of minor importance. But the sketch-work and measuring preparatory to them imparted to Seddon a thorough familiarity with the Welsh medieval country church and, he would later recall, a deep admiration for 'these modest churches, their simplicity was so different from the comparative pretentiousness of modern work generally and even of old work in richer districts elsewhere. I have often tried, in consequence, to work on the same general lines'.[10]

Seddon was also given charge at Llandaff of the new cathedral fittings, and seized upon this opportunity to implement his philosophy of 'unity in the arts' by commissioning several of their elements from his friends in the Pre-Raphaelite Brotherhood.[11] Seddon's friendship with the Pre-Raphaelites – Brown, Hunt and Rossetti in particular – stemmed from his brother Thomas's close relationship with the group, which itself had begun around 1848–9 when Thomas was studying at Charles Lucy's School of Drawing and Modelling in Camden Town. Brown and Rossetti soon became family friends, frequently socialising with J. P. and his siblings or dining at the elder Thomas Seddon's home in Highgate. It was an enduring friendship, too: much later, in 1882,

Fig. 2: Plate VII from Progress in Art and Architecture ... . *More details from Early French Gothic architecture in Normandy. The capital on the hooked shaft (top left) is from Coutances Cathedral, and was one of Seddon's favourite devices, featuring in churches from the 1850s (e.g. Llandogo) through to the 1880s (e.g. Grangetown, Cardiff).*

Seddon offered free use of Westcliffe, one of his new bungalows at Birchington-on-Sea, Kent, to William Rossetti, who was seeking a place of convalescence for his seriously ill brother, Dante Gabriel.[12]

The various PRB projects for Llandaff Cathedral were initiated over the course of 1855–6, and the process seems to have underscored in Seddon's mind the necessity of widening the exposure of his and Prichard's practice. The firm subsequently entered two high-profile competitions, for the Crimea Memorial Church, and the War and Foreign Offices, both announced in the late summer of 1856. Seddon also ceased to be so ambivalent toward the Ecclesiological Society's policies, recognising the power wielded by the group's journal, *The Ecclesiologist*. He began attending society meetings to present his and Prichard's designs[13] and joined in November 1857. Then, early in 1858, Seddon opened the partnership's London office, a new cosmopolitan base from which he was able to launch his own personal bid for a greater professional reputation and a long career amongst the luminaries of High Victorian Gothic.

Church beginnings and rise to prominence

As noted, Seddon's first ecclesiastical designs were for minor restorations in Monmouthshire, where Prichard had simply been unable to keep up with the necessary repairs to the county's many dilapidated parish churches. These jobs were ideally suited to the novice Seddon in that they allowed him to begin working creatively in the Gothic style on isolated elements such as bell-cotes, porches, or tracery. As such, he was able to experiment rather freely with various Gothic precedents while searching for his own distinctive style.

Seddon soon settled into using the Ecclesiology-approved Decorated style, and this is plainly evident in his earliest known design for a new church, from 1854, an unsuccessful competition entry for Holy Trinity, Tulse Hill in south London.[14] Equally so, however, is Seddon's immaturity, such that each pattern of window tracery was different, as were the several spirelet designs, the gable crosses and piercings, the various buttress profiles. But some features that would characterise Seddon's churches over the coming decades made their debut here, while others reveal that he was an early believer in looking beyond England and to the continent for inspiration.[15] Seddon's preference was for the Gothic of Normandy, an affinity which would likewise surface later to become a distinguishing feature of his churches.

It was not long before Seddon's skills matured sufficiently for the realisation of thoroughly unified compositions and the emergence of a truly personal style. In a group of new churches in the diocese of Llandaff designed from 1857 one may note the very simple Geometric tracery, early French foliate capitals, and the introduction of constructional polychromy. The late appearance of this last feature in Seddon's ecclesiastical work is purely down to want of opportunity, for he had been using polychromy in his domestic designs for some years. However, it is worth noting that the mix of colour in his ecclesiastical work tended to be gentler and more subtle. The Monmouthshire churches of Pontnewydd (1857) and Llandogo (1858, Fig. 3) – 'a lovely little church' Seddon called it[16] – are both good examples of the delight Seddon took in exploiting a variety of textures and hues for his wall fabric. There can be little doubt that it was Prichard's talent and enthusiasm for conspicuously local materials that was guiding Seddon at this point through the practicalities of his masonry techniques.[17] But as always with Seddon, the counsel

Fig. 3: Llandogo, St Odoceus, Monmouthshire, 1858, west end. Seddon identified this church as one of his most successful and favourite buildings – 'a lovely little church', he remarked in a 1902 interview with A. Wilcox, published as 'Interview with Mr. John P. Seddon, F.R.I.B.A. An architect of many churches', Church Bells & Illustrated Church News *32 (1902), 141-2 (141). (Author)*

of Ruskin was never far away. Writing in 1863 about stone construction, Seddon reiterated and expanded upon Ruskin's belief that the ultimate value of a building lay in the undisguised display of the architect's thought and devotion to his craft.[18] 'The evidence of thought', he wrote, ' is more precious than that of labour. Above all, do not be cheese-paring with thought. Consider thoroughly the purpose and position each stone is to perform and to occupy...look how it was done in the good old days of Gothic architecture, and do likewise.'[19]

Such commentary by Seddon routinely supplemented the built expressions of his architectural theories. In fact, only during his first years in Wales as Prichard's partner was there any marked hiatus in the vigorous stream of lectures, books and essays that poured from his pen. Still, this break was addressed immediately on Seddon's return to London in 1858 when he began to make his presence known at the current forums of architectural discourse.[20] Now aged 31, he was confident, even brazen in his outspoken conviction in the superiority of the Gothic style, and his incisively witty lectures were often quick to spark lively debate on their more controversial assertions. 'What did Mr. Seddon mean by playing *high jinks* in his lecture?' asked the *Building News* after Seddon's first London talk following his return. 'He has a fling at caryatides, which he terms a *freak*, yet shuts his eyes to ... far more offensive Gothic *freaks*'.[21] Seddon was elected to RIBA fellowship in 1860 (he had been an associate since 1852), and new positions of responsibility followed, the most prestigious of which was as honorary secretary to the RIBA which he held from 1862 to 1871. But he was also a founding member of the Medieval Society, on the committees of the Architectural Publication Society and Architectural Photographic Association, and a member of the council for the Architectural Exhibition.

Through all these endeavours, Seddon placed himself firmly at the forefront of the Gothic Revival's most aggressive factions. A member of what the *Building News* described as 'the rising school of Gothic architects',[22] he reconnected on his return to London with Pre-Raphaelite friends Rossetti and Brown, as well as becoming very close to Burges and Godwin.[23] From 1858, Seddon was also actively pursuing an association with Hart & Son, intent on securing quality metalwork for his buildings. Contracts for tiles from Godwin's of Lugwardine, glass from Morris, Marshall, Faulkner & Co., and, of course, furniture made by his family firm followed shortly after, all indicative of Seddon's Reformed Gothic philosophy of 'unity in the arts'. Thus as High Victorian Gothic swelled to become the dominant architectural force, Seddon was resolutely ensconced at the movement's heart, and poised to emerge as one of its most tenacious proponents.

Career heights and the Muscular Gothic style

At the start of the 1860s, then, the beginnings of Seddon's personal style had fully materialised, rooted in his dedication to Ruskin and fondness of the unpretentious simplicity of rural Welsh prototypes. His ecclesiastical output still largely comprised restorations, but new churches such as St John, Templeton in Pembrokeshire, and St John the Evangelist at Maindee in Newport, both of 1859, clearly expressed Seddon's design philosophy. Stonework was quoined and banded with various colours, windows were filled with simple Geometrical patterns worked in bar tracery, and decorative detail was richly naturalistic. All of these guiding principles now merged readily with the dawning taste for robust 'muscularity', and set Seddon's ecclesiastical work in a fresh direction. First seen in the detailing of an unexecuted design for St Andrew's, Cardiff, of 1859,[24] this new path was more boldly explored a year later at the church of St Margaret, Mountain Ash in Glamorgan. Its most distinctive and obviously novel attribute was the proliferation of chunky plate tracery, specifically chosen by Seddon on the basis of cost. Explaining this to the Incorporated Church Building Society, Seddon wrote that he had 'endeavoured to work out with ecclesiastical effect what may be deemed rather an improvement on the temporary churches usually considered sufficient in such cases'.[25] However for Seddon, what ultimately sprang from this tangible exercise in cost control was aesthetic appreciation of much more primitive Gothic forms; and, it was the uniform application of these forms that came to define his ecclesiastical style during the early years of his professional independence, outside the sphere of Prichard's influence and in touch with the developing continental flavour of High Victorian Gothic.

Seddon's first thorough demonstration of this new brand of Gothic was his unsuccessful competition entry for Cork Cathedral in 1862.[26] Early Gothic was the specified style and the majority of competitors – Seddon and the victorious Burges included – opted for a predominantly French aspect in their designs.[27] Seddon drew heavily on the Norman precedents with which he was familiar, such as Caen for the crossing tower, Bayeux for the tracery, and Norrey for the flanking turrets. But he also included a band of pictorial mosaics above the nave arcades, in the Italo-Byzantine tradition, as well as drawing inspiration from the First Pointed of his native England, by introducing ringed shafts and a set of triple lancets on the west front.

All Saints, Chigwell Row, Essex, begun in 1866, exhibits much of the spirit of Seddon's Cork designs, with its bold plate tracery and rugged cast (Fig. 4). As built, it is missing several of the more overt and accomplished continental references originally

Fig. 4: Chigwell Row, All Saints, Essex, 1866-7, west end. Seddon nearly lost this commission due to the costly nature of his first two designs. The church as built is much simplified from his original proposals, and the tower and chancel were built independently in 1903 and 1918 respectively. (Author)

proposed, particularly the Italianate system of decoration Seddon continued to favour, in which structural polychromy was combined with designated areas of pictorial art. Strict budget regulation also prevented Seddon from using a more extensive array of plate tracery patterns than he would have liked although he succeeded in adorning the church with lush Early French carving.

All Saints was Seddon's first new church following the dissolution of his partnership with Prichard in early 1863. Their split had not been amicable. It was initiated by Seddon after Prichard had abandoned him late in 1862 to consult on a job in southern Spain, leaving Seddon to resolve hostilities which had arisen at Ettington Park, Warwickshire, between Prichard, his builder, Thomas Williams, and the patron, E. P. Shirley.[28] But the prospect of a break-up had probably been on Seddon's mind for some time, his own aspirations lying well beyond the regional confines of South Wales, with this incident just serving as a convenient excuse. Prichard felt painfully betrayed and although he and Seddon were later able to renew their professional friendship, Prichard requested that on his death his most recent partner, F. R. Kempson (1837 or '38–1923), should succeed him as diocesan architect and not Seddon. It was an awkward situation for Seddon when he applied for the post regardless, in search of a comfortable and secure twilight to his career.[29]

Such concerns, however, could not have been further from Seddon's mind in the mid-1860s. His practice was expanding, now based in the smart residential district of Park Street, Westminster. In 1864, he married Margaret Barber, cousin of W. S.

Barber, a mutual friend of his and Burges's whom they knew through the Architectural Photographic Association.[30] As the RIBA grew in size and stature, so too did Seddon's responsibilities and reputation as its honorary secretary. He wrote copiously for the professional journals and gave frequent lectures to his peers as well as students of the Architectural Association.[31] Always replete with clever satire, these many essays pointedly articulated Seddon's self-confidence and buoyant determination to advance the Gothic cause. 'As to the ... *classic malady*,' he declared at a RIBA lecture in 1864, 'it is much to be feared that it has brought its adherents into a state of atrophy, and the most strenuous efforts are still imperatively called for ... to prevent the spread of its cankering disease'. But Seddon was quick to condemn what he felt were ill-conceived interpretations of the Gothic Revival as well. He pilloried the excessive use of crockets, stripes and pinnacles, designating it as the '*hair-stand-on-end-style*', and despaired of the '*galvanized glove-stretcher mania* ... caught from a too close study of Early Gothic foliage ... If we would only condescend to be simple and true', he concluded, 'thinking less of ourselves and our reputation and more of our work for its own sake'.[32]

Seddon's unswerving architectural doctrine also found expression in the many church restoration projects he had in hand, which were generally founded on the correction of their style and space. At St Nicholas, Great Yarmouth, for example, he removed much of the Perpendicular tracery which he 'deeply ... regretted as marring the nobler work of the earlier periods' and replaced it with completely conjectural Geometrical windows.[33] Later, under fire from the SPAB for such work, Seddon boldly crowed, 'I am a hardened sinner, for I glory in my crime ... to trample on the wretched ... Georgian *neat and elegant*, ... to have torn down rubbish and rebuilt ruins'.[34]

All Saints, Chigwell Row was the last of Seddon's larger churches to show any strong links to the Ecclesiological preference for traditional aisled naves with deep, separate chancels, for toward the end of the decade, he began to show an interest in solving the problems posed by town church planning by opening up the nave space after basilican or friary church models. Ten years earlier, he and Prichard had pioneered the use of narrow passage aisles in designs for St Andrew's, Cardiff. A device that would later prove very popular in church planning,[35] the evidence suggests that Seddon conceived it in the process of rearranging the seats at Llantilio Crosseny, Monmouthshire, in 1856. Here, he determined to do away with the central aisle altogether and provide access to seats only along the perimeter of the nave, in order to address the difficulties of viewing the altar through the very low crossing arches.[36] However, Seddon did not have another opportunity to explore truly innovative spatial exercises until Victorian architects generally were re-assessing their church planning strategies, swept up by the need to address contemporary challenges to both the design and decoration of conventional High Victorian places of Anglican worship.[37] Several adventurous schemes from the late 1860s revealed Seddon's enthusiastic support for aspects of this movement.[38] Most striking of these was that for St James, Great Yarmouth, from 1869 (Fig. 5), where Seddon broke sharply with customary practice by proposing a vast crossing dome, clearly after the Venetian traditions in which he still found inspiration.[39]

Consistency in the face of change

St James's sits at a crossroads in Seddon's career, in that it was designed just as architectural fashion was shifting away from the massive and foreign and toward something more delicate and perceived as more English. To some extent, this change was a

Fig. 5: Great Yarmouth, St. James, 1868-78. Interior perspective of crossing from The Architect, 28 *(1882), plate following p. 346. Although this magnificent domed crossing was reported quite unambiguously as built in* Building News, 34 (1878), 481-2, *there is absolutely no trace of it today.*

reaction to the muscular Gothic dominance of the 1866 competition for the new Royal Courts of Justice. Seddon was one of twelve architects invited to compete and predicted by the *Building News* as one of the five likely to produce the winning scheme.[40] His design, which featured an audaciously tall record tower and central hall of equally large proportions, proved to be very popular with the general public for its daring demeanour. However, it was also conspicuously rife with the excesses of colossal scale which were soon to become the butt of professional critique, as architects both young and old struggled to find a vocabulary more appropriate to contemporary British life.

There is just an inkling at St James's of a cautious response from Seddon to this new trend, via its flint and brick construction and later Decorated tracery, both of which referred to recognisably English traditions. But for the most part, Seddon remained resistant to the tides of change washing over his profession during the 1870s. This was largely down to the continued supply of reliably long-term and strictly High Gothic Revival commissions which dominated his workload from 1864 through to the mid-1880s, and sheltered him from the pressure to change tack. Three were large scale and complex church restorations – Grosmont, Monmouthshire; Llanbadarn Fawr, Cardiganshire; and St Nicholas, Great Yarmouth. There was also the Castle House Hotel in Aberystwyth (later University College Wales), an imposing, fairy-tale château based on Viollet-le-Duc's publications and the Rhenish architecture Seddon himself promoted in his 1868 book *Rambles in the Rhine Provinces*. Lastly, from 1867, Seddon was the chosen architect of Catharine Tait, wife of A. C. Tait, the archbishop of Canterbury from 1868. Until her death in 1878, Mrs. Tait specifically gave or contrived nine substantial commissions for Seddon, ranging from labourers' dwellings, to church restorations, to an orphanage and schools. All of them gratified their shared devotion to the High Victorian Gothic style, just as its wider appeal was waning.

Active as he was at the top echelon of the profession's administrative body, as well as in many subsidiary organisations, Seddon was by no means unaware of the changes in taste which were afoot on the wider stage. Certainly he made vociferous and quarrelsome attacks on current attempts to forge a new, non-Gothic style. 'Would-be architectural reformers ... clamour for new styles,' he remarked disdainfully in 1872, still confident that the recent experiments in 'a hybrid of the most corrupt versions of the Renaissance' could not pose much challenge to Gothic.[41] Three years later, Seddon remained defiant, despite the evidence in his midst:

There was no point of merit or interest in the work of Queen Anne's time that was original, inherent, or due to the style. There was no style whatever about it. The few desirable points which it possessed...[are] wholly independent of the senseless, trashy nature of the details used. Let architects go back,...to that whence it derived all that it had of inspiration, and beyond that whence it got all its impurity and absurdity. And whither should we go but to Gothic?[42]

Seddon was fortunate that the resilience of his Gothic Revival faith during this period of stylistic evolution found favour for the above mentioned jobs. He was also lucky that his reputation and patronage network brought instructions for three significant new churches in 1873–4, at the height of the revolt against Muscular Gothic. Each one was a truly *bijou* creation and permitted Seddon to revel in the genres of ecclesiastical design he loved best.

At Ullenhall, Warwickshire, having designed the vicarage, Seddon was next asked to build St Mary's church (Fig. 6). Its complex exterior profile reflects the playful mix of basic geometric shapes which Seddon devised for the plan,[43] while a carefully crafted array of golden Campden stone gives the walls a subtle polychromy. Seddon's customary early Geometrical tracery

Fig. 6: Ullenhall, St Mary, Warwickshire, 1874-5, from the north-west. Built for the Newton family of nearby Barrell's Park where Seddon later designed a 'Winter Garden'. This church was one of Seddon's most completely realised designs, incorporating details sourced from his favourite continental precedents. (Author)

then combines with other favourite devices of his: the Transitional apse with its arcaded corbel table and smooth sweep, an octagonal Rhineland spire, and Norman arcading along the internal walls.

Designed simultaneously but starkly different in outward appearance is the polychromatic brick church of Ayot St Peter in Hertfordshire (Fig. 7). Seddon won this commission in a competition to replace a Pearson church recently destroyed by fire although why Pearson was not called back is not clear. Seddon's church seems to be fairly similar to Pearson's original building,

Fig. 7: Ayot St Peter, St Peter, Hertfordshire, 1874-5, east end. Another of Seddon's most thoroughly fulfilled projects in which he was able to showcase some of his most recent decorative arts ventures in glass, mosaic, tiles and stoneware. (Author)

which was apparently a red-brick version of his Early French Christ Church at Appleton-le-Moors, North Yorkshire.[44] Certainly Seddon's design looks back to the exuberant patterning and continental detail that were in vogue ten to fifteen years earlier. Inside, he indulged in further splendid colours, both reflecting the exterior and as a foil to the rugged early thirteenth-century tracery. Seddon intended the nave walls to be faced in Rust's mosaics, regrettably never executed. Otherwise, most of his richly vibrant decorative programme was installed: a painted ceiling by J. R. Thompson, unique stoneware chancel arch by the Fulham Pottery, Rust's mosaic font and floor, and stained glass by H. A. Kennedy.

Perhaps the most unusual church of Seddon's career is St Catherine's, Hoarwithy in Herefordshire, built from 1873 for his good friend the Revd William Poole of nearby Hentland (Figs. 8 & 9).[45] Its thoroughly Romanesque aspect might easily be mistaken for an attempt by Seddon at the *Rundbogenstil*, increasingly popular in the early 1870s. However, it was Poole himself who explicitly ordained the sources Seddon was to follow, namely the twelfth-century architecture of northern Italy and France.[46] Of course these were styles Seddon could easily work with, having studied and admired many of their examples during his travels, and he clearly delighted in extrapolating Poole's directives to include manifestations of his own preferred models. Thus we see a Venetian campanile, early Lombard or Byzantine capitals,[47] an apse cornice and corbel table after Laach and other

Fig. 8: Hoarwithy, St Catherine, Herefordshire, 1872-83. From the south, showing the claustral approach. Seddon's only Romanesque Revival church, built for his friend of many years, the Revd William Poole. Seddon's building encased a brick chapel of c.1840, and featured an array of Venetian and Lombard interior decorations based on those he had seen and drawn during his 1851, post-articles tour of the continent. (Author)

Fig. 9: Hoarwithy, St Catherine. Detail of cloister capitals. (Author)

Rhineland churches,[48] and fanciful grotesques in the manner of both continental Romanesque and the nearby church of Kilpeck.

Later churches

In 1880, Seddon was unanimously appointed architect for the new parish church of St Paul, Hammersmith. Desirous of obtaining an edifice to rival G. G. Scott's nearby St Mary Abbotts, Kensington, of 1869–72, the working committee decided to eschew competition and directly employ an architect who 'had made Ecclesiastical architecture his special study and training and had also attained a position of approved eminence in his profession'.[49]

St Paul's was unusual in Seddon's oeuvre at this date, particularly in its overall impression of soaring height. But this can be ascribed to Seddon's collaborator and friend, Hugh Roumieu Gough (c.1842–1904). It was Gough, Seddon later explained, who had engineered a concealed iron roof as a cheap solution to the problem of ensuring a vaulted ceiling alongside the requisite 'lofty proportions', yet with little or no thrust on the clerestory and no transverse ties. Seddon also made clear in this report that his preferred remedy to this problem would not have used a sham structure,[50] a point of principle which possibly precipitated Gough's increasing responsibility for the works.[51] This is not to deprive Seddon of all credit for St Paul's, for many of its elements were clearly down to his creativity and inclinations: the arcaded clerestory, the Rhenish spirelets and gable piercing and the low narrow aisles. But one may equally look to Gough's churches of St Cuthbert, Kensington (1884), and St Dunstan, Liverpool (1885), for an indication not only of what he must have gleaned from Hammersmith, but also what he probably contributed to its final incarnation.

What one *can* be certain of is that Seddon's experience at

Hammersmith convinced him of the potential of Early English as a working style. He had used it before, sparingly, at his Mountain Ash church, in the Cork design, and in several schools. Now Seddon embraced it with enthusiasm, delighting in its rhythmic vistas of lancets and pure, basic forms. It also answered the calls for an architecture reflective of native rather than foreign traditions, and better suited Seddon's preference for a meatier, more tectonic treatment of the wall surface than did the diaphanous planes and spindly tracery of the contemporary Perpendicular Revival. Gorse Hill, Swindon (1883), New Tredegar (1890) and Briton Ferry (1891), both in Glamorgan, partook of this spirit, low but spacious hall churches, outwardly brusque and tough in their detail.

Seddon's other common formula for church design toward the end of his career resurrected the breadth he had originally sought at St James, Great Yarmouth. It also revived his penchant for bold Geometric tracery, continental references and variety in the texture and colour of wall surfaces. St Andrew, Redruth in Cornwall (1880–84), was particularly remarkable for its return to techniques used by Prichard and Seddon in the 1850s – the parcelling up of the wall and heavy West Country tracery – all the more so as it was designed simultaneously with Hammersmith. At St Paul, Grangetown, Cardiff (1888: Fig. 10) and All Saints, Penarth, Glamorgan (1889), enormous full-height, cross-gabled aisles dominate both the north and south elevations. They are filled with very tall, slim two-light windows reminiscent of Rhenish and Low Country examples.

In 1884, Seddon took his former improver, John Coates Carter (1859–1927) into partnership. In so doing, Seddon was able to open an office in Cardiff and begin to re-establish himself in South Wales where his early career had blossomed so profitably.

Fig. 10: Grangetown, Cardiff, St Paul, 1888-1902, north side. Designed with John Coates Carter, this vast hall church was intended to compete in scale and grandeur with Bodley & Garner's nearby St German's (1881-4). The walls are faced, as Seddon liked, with rubble divided into compartments by dressed stone, although the dressings here include Portland cement blocks, curiously speckled with small pink pebbles. (Author)

Grangetown and Penarth were both part of the new stream of Welsh ecclesiastical commissions that came into this office, though it is worth noting that there was no noticeable increase in such jobs until after the death of John Prichard in 1886. Carter went on to become one of the region's most important Arts and Crafts architects, and although his later church work diverged sharply from Seddon's, something of Seddon's influence would seem to have survived in the unaffected simplicity of his forms and uncompromising solidity of his wall structure.

With Carter's aid, then, Seddon was able to continue growing his practice right up until the end of his life, all the while never flinching from his devout observance of the Gothic Revival creed. 'All the world knows Mr. J. P. Seddon to be an able architect who has withstood all the *fashions*', Raffles Davison had written in 1881, 'and, firm to his faith in English Gothic, designs yesterday, to-day, and in the future, what he himself thinks best'.[52] True to this prediction, Seddon was supervising the rebuilding of the south transept at Chepstow Priory as late as 1904. It is an austere and powerful addition to the grand Romanesque core, nonetheless worked confidently in his favourite Geometrical style.

Seddon's output – which spanned more than fifty years and ran to well over 200 building projects – may be divided roughly equally between ecclesiastical and secular works. However, it is as a church architect that Seddon was known in later life[53] and is primarily remembered today. How then to assess his ecclesiastical designs in relation to the dynamic Victorian architectural traditions of which they were a part? Central to this question is the fact that Seddon was guided by very broad principles: the simplicity of decorative forms, the honest expression of masonry and construction, and the absolute necessity that design be, as he put it in 1880, 'modified with common-sense to modern requirements...and perfect adaptation to the wants of the day'.[54] It is true that Seddon's own relentless use of thirteenth-century precedents might seem at odds with such a modern overarching philosophy; and it is possible that his stubbornly immutable design vocabulary is partly responsible for his relative obscurity today. But it is testimony to the importance of Seddon's ideologies that we so often and easily perceive them in the works of his most celebrated pupil, C. F. A. Voysey, who was in Seddon's office from 1874 until 1879.

On his death in 1906, at the age of seventy-eight, Seddon was generally acknowledged to have been 'one of the last survivors of the Gothic Revival' as his obituary in the *Building News* remarked.[55] It was an epitaph he had already come to accept in the final decades of his life, happily persevering with what *The*

Architect said 'to him was more than a style; it was an artistic faith'.[56] Indeed, Seddon's zealous devotion to High Victorian Gothic was never confined to those decades of its greatest popularity, as was the case with so many others of his generation. And, the thoroughness with which Seddon's designs consistently embodied the movement's principles, combined with the clarity and eloquence of his polemics, is what makes him such an important and fascinating representative of the period.

Notes

1 'Church Architecture', read to the Church Congress at Leeds, 2 October 1872, and printed in *The Architect*, 8 (1872), 199–202.

2 Seddon's obituaries are in *The Architect*, 75 (1906), 89; *The Builder,* 90 (1906), 150; *Building News*, 90 (1906), 203; and *Journal of the R.I.B.A.,* 3rd ser.,13 (1905–6), 194, 221. See also J. P. Seddon, *Memoir and Letters of the Late Thomas Seddon, artist* (London, 1858), 2.

3 Seddon, *Memoir*, 5 and 10. Donaldson's obituaries are in *The Builder*, 49 (1885), 179–8; (1885), 212–4; and *Transactions of the R.I.B.A.*, n.s. 2 (1885–6), 89–108.

4 Obituary of Donaldson in *Transactions of the R.I.B.A.*, 94.

5 Childhood and youth experiences from *Memoir*, 1–7; and William Rossetti (ed.), *Preraphaellite Diaries and Letters* (London, 1900), 104–5, 108–9, and 161. For specific quote on Seddon's mistrust of the Roman Catholic church, *see* e.g. his paper 'Art in Relation to Architecture', *Civil Engineer & Architect's Journal*, 29 (1866), 89–91 (91).

6 Seddon, 'Progress in Architecture', *The Builder*, 8 (1850), 124–5; 'Notes of a Tour among the Cathedrals and Churches of Brittany and Normandy', *Civil Engineer & Architect's Journal*, 14 (1851), 553; 'Critical Remarks upon some of the Monuments at Venice and in other Places on the Route thither', *The Builder*, 10 (1852), 310–11. Also Seddon, 'The Late John Prichard', *Proceedings of the R.I.B.A.*, n.s. 3 (1886), 81–3.

7 His first office address was at Percy Chambers, 7 Percy Street, Tottenham Court Road, where he shared the premises with his older brother Thomas and fellow A.R.I.B.A. Alfred Bailey (*fl.* 1851–6). Prior to this, in 1850, Seddon had designed a parsonage at Lacey Green, Buckinghamshire (he would add a chancel to the church in 1870–2) but he was at this time still articled to Donaldson He completed his articles in May 1851 before setting off on a three-month tour of Flanders, the Rhine and finally northern Italy.

8 Seddon, 'The Works of the PRB in Llandaff Cathedral', *Cardiff Public Library Journal*, 4 (1903–4), 28–9.

9 Seddon, 'The Late John Prichard', 82.

10 Seddon, 'On Sundry Working Drawings', read to the Architectural Association on 24 November 1882 and printed in the *British Architect*, 18 (1882), 584–7 (586) and 621–4.

11 Seddon, 'The Works of the PRB in Llandaff Cathedral', 29. For his underlying philosophy in unity amongst the several branches of art, see his first publication *Progress in Art and Architecture with Precedents for Ornament* (London, 1852), 17.

12 Seddon, *Memoir*, esp. 6–20, 139 and 171; Rossetti (ed.), *Preraphaellite Diaries and Letters,* esp. 27–33, 104–14, 144 and 161–99; George P. Landau, 'William Holman Hunt's Letters to Thomas Seddon', *Bulletin of the John Rylands University Library of Manchester*, 66 (Autumn 1983), 139–72; and Angela Thirlwell, *William and Lucy: The Other Rossettis* (London, 2003), 59, 91–2, 102–4 and 289.

13 Seddon's first reported attendance at an Ecclesiological Society meeting in *The Ecclesiologist,* 17 (1856), 297. Regular reports on Prichard and Seddon designs begin to appear in the journal from 1857.

14 Drawings held in the V&A Print Room d.713–19.1896.

15 For discussion of Norman influences on the Gothic Revival generally see Gavin Stamp, 'High Victorian Gothic and the Architecture of Normandy', *Society of Architectural Historians Journal,* 62 (2003), 194–211. The newness of interest in continental Gothic is discussed in G. E. Street, 'The True Principles of Architecture and the Possibility of Development', read to the Oxford Architectural Society, 18 February 1852 and printed in *The Ecclesiologist,* 13 (1852), 247–62.

16 Quoted in A. Wilcox, 'Interview with Mr. John P. Seddon, F.R.I.B.A. An Architect of many Churches', *Church Bells & Illustrated Church News,* 32 (1902), 141–2 (141).

17 Seddon, 'The Late John Prichard', 82; and letter from Seddon to the *Western Mail* (18 October 1886), reprinted in the *Building News,* 51 (1886), 604.

18 *The Stones of Venice* I (1851), 37; and 'The Lamp of Life', in *The Seven Lamps of Architecture* (1849).

19 'Some practical remarks upon wall masonry', *Civil Engineer & Architect's Journal,* 26 (1863), 192–3 (193).

20 Seddon, 'Ancient and Modern Ornament Contrasted', *Building News,* 4 (1858), 109–12. Seddon attended the first Architectural Association Conversazione for the 1858–9 session and commented on how good it was to be back in London, as reported in the *Building News,* 4 (1858), 1005.

21 'Chips of Criticism', *Building News,* 4 (1858), 148, comments on Seddon's 'Ancient and Modern Ornament' paper cited in note 20.

22 7 (1861), 406.

23 The list of publicised references to shared interests, activities and collaborations is lengthy. But of particular note from the Seddon family bible, now in the possession of Jeremy Seddon (great-grandson of Seddon's younger brother Henry Cooper Seddon), is that Burges was one of Seddon's groomsmen and Godwin attended the christening of Seddon's youngest daughter.

24 Drawings held in the V&A Print Room d.744, 746–9.1896.

25 Incorporated Church Building Society papers, Lambeth Palace Library, file 5659.

26 Drawings held in the V&A Print Room d.791–805.1896.

27 *Building News,* 10 (1863), 329. See also *Building News,* 8 (1862), 315; *The Ecclesiologist,* 24 (1863), 164; and *The Builder,* 21 (1863), 217.

28 Geoffrey Tyack, 'A Victorian Architectural Correspondence', *Architectural History,* 22 (1979), 78–87 (at 85); and Seddon, 'The Late John Prichard', 82–3.

29 Letter from Prichard to Seddon, 19 January 1871, and held in the John Rylands Library, University of Manchester; letter from Seddon to the diocese of Llandaff held in the National Library of Wales, Schedule of Church in Wales Records LL/Ch/3314; and O. Jenkins, 'Illustrative Examples of the Effect on Medieval and later Parish Church Fabric in the post 1844 Archdeaconry of Llandaff of Restoration Work by John Prichard and John Pollard Seddon', Architectural Association thesis (1995), 124–5.

30 Barber drew some of the plates for Burges's *Architectural Drawings* (London, 1870).

31 Between 1863 and 1870, Seddon wrote or presented 39 papers and commented/wrote published letters on 67 separate occasions.

32 'Sundry Notes upon some Miscellaneous Subjects', read at the R.I.B.A. by C. F. Hayward in Seddon's absence, 15 February 1864, and printed in *Transactions of the R.I.B.A.,* 1st ser. 14 (1863–4), xxi–xxvi (xxii–xxiii).

33 Seddon, 'St Nicholas Church, Great Yarmouth', read to the R.I.B.A., 6 February 1865, and printed in *Transactions of the R.I.B.A.,* 1st Ser., 15 (1864–5), 75–84 (83).

34 'A Defense of Restoration', *Ecclesiastical Art Review* (March 1878), 44–6 (45–6).

35 For recent discussion see Geoffrey K. Brandwood, *Temple Moore: An Architect of the Late Gothic Revival* (Stamford, 1997), 46–53; and Anthony Symondson, 'Theology, Worship and the Late Victorian Church', in Chris Brooks and Andrew. Saint (eds.), *The Victorian Church* (Manchester, 1995), 192–222 (201–3).

36 Incorporated Church Building Society papers, Lambeth Palace Library, file 5011. Seddon, 'Church architecture', 200, refers to Prichard and Seddon's early use of the system.

37 The architectural press was full of commentary on the subject: *Building News,* 18

(1870), 352; 21 (1871), 309; *The Architect,* 8 (1872), 86–7; *British Architect,* 1 (1874), 207. The best contemporary summary of the movement is in James Cubitt, *Church Designs for Congregations: Its Developments and Possibilities* (London, 1869). See also E. C. Robins, 'Congregational Church Building', read to the Architectural Association, 14 November 1873, in *The Architect,* 10 (1873), 284. More recently, Symondson, 'Theology, Worship and the Late Victorian Church'. Seddon co-judged a town church competition organised by the *Building News* and reported in 25 (1873), 109–10, 142–5.

38 Failed competition entries for St Swithin's, Lincoln, and St Mary's, Slough, both of 1868, featured enormous nave spans bounded by narrow aisles and with huge clerestory windows.

39 The dome is not extant, and it is unclear whether it was ever built.

40 14 (1867), 57–8. The other four favourites were Scott, Street, Waterhouse and Burges.

41 Seddon, 'The Style for the Future', *Building News,* 23 (1872), 227.

42 Comments on H. H. Stannus's paper 'The *Queen Anne* movement, and its relationship to Gothic and Classic', read to the Architectural Association, 17 April 1875, and printed in the *Building News,* 28 (1875), 456–7.

43 This use of geometric shapes was commented on at the time in the *British Architect,* 17 (1877), 316.

44 Anthony Quiney, *John Loughborough Pearson* (New Haven & London, 1979), 240.

45 Seddon first met Poole in 1854 when he arrived in Hentland as the new vicar and commissioned the redecoration of its chancel. Seddon went on to build Poole's new vicarage and school, plus other schools in the area at Poole's instigation. Poole's niece, Madeline Hopton, wrote that Seddon was a 'great friend' of her uncle, in *Records of Hentland Parish,* typescript in the Hopton Collection of Hereford Public Library (1916), 85.

46 Hopton, *Records,* 87–91.

47 See drawings by Seddon of San Vitale and San Marco held in the V&A Print Room d.1171.1907 and d.1109.1907 respectively.

48 Seddon praised this feature of Laach as one of the best in Transitional architecture of the Rhine in *Rambles in the Rhine Provinces* (London, 1868), 24–5, 69.

49 St Paul, Hammersmith, parish records: committee minutes as reported in R. Lee and M. Harris, *History and Guide to the Parish Church of St Paul's Hammersmith* (London 1984). Lee and Harris were confused by the committee's choice of Seddon, typically unaware of how well-respected he was at that time.

50 Seddon, 'Sundry Working Drawings', 621–2.

51 By 1883 Gough is referred to first in accounts, and in 1889 on completion of the tower, Gough is the only architect mentioned by the *Ecclesiastical Arts Gazette* (November 1889), 23.

52 'On Pictorial Effects in Drawing', *British Architect,* 17 (1881), 173.

53 Wilcox, 'Interview'.

54 Letter on the Bedford Park Estate to the *Building News,* 38 (1880), 178.

55 90 (1906), 203.

56 75 (1906), 89.

George Fellowes Prynne (1853–1927): a dedicated life

Ruth Sharville

GEORGE HALFORD FELLOWES PRYNNE (Fig. 1) was born on 2 April 1853 at Wyndham Square, Plymouth, Devon. He was the second son of the Revd George Rundle Prynne (1818–1903) and Emily Fellowes. As well as his elder brother, the artist Edward Alfred, he had another brother, Albert Bernard (known as Bernard), and two sisters.

George Rundle Prynne was a staunch supporter of the Oxford Movement and a well-known activist in religious circles. His church, St Peter's, was one with a strong sense of mission, and Prynne senior was heavily involved in education, ministry to the sick, supporting the poor and preaching the gospel. He was aided

Ruth Sharville is a civil servant who has taken an interest in the work of George Fellowes Prynne since her days as a chorister at both St Peter's, Staines, and All Saints, West Dulwich.

Fig. 1: George Fellowes Prynne. Photograph printed from a glass negative. (Fellowes-Prynne family collection)

by a community of sisters, on whom fell much of the burden of the day-to-day work of the church in what was a very deprived area. Very little information is available about the young George's childhood. However, he cannot have failed to be influenced by his father's indomitable spirit and tireless work ethic.

George Fellowes Prynne, as he was known throughout his life, was sent away to school, first of all to St Mary's College, Harlow, then Chardstock College, Dorset, and finally to Eastman's Royal Naval Academy at Southsea. An impression of his life as a young man can be obtained from biographical notes, which were compiled on his 44th birthday in 1897 by his secretary and subsequently checked by him.[1] In these he mentioned that his first interest in the study of architecture was inspired by the books of Thomas Rickman and J. H. Parker, to which he had access when his eldest brother, Edward, was studying with a view to entering the office of George Edmund Street, a friend of his father. However, he stated that his main desire was to be ordained, and he spent some time studying privately with a tutor near Oxford with this in view, but, as he put it, 'difficulties arose as to the expense of a University education'. His notes then describe the next turn of events which, extraordinarily, took him in 1871 to what was still the Wild West and all its rigours:

> At the age of 18 … an offer came from an uncle, to get me a berth with a nephew of his who had taken land, and was farming in the Western states of America. I started on my new life's career. The experience of Western farming life was both trying and severe, especially during the last nine months of the nearly 2 years spent in the then wild West. 26 years ago the states of Iowa and Nebraska presented a very different aspect to what they do at present….
>
> The life and living generally was of the roughest. Many of the Englishmen farming in those parts were of a rough hardened 'dare-devil' sort. It was here that one learnt to face difficulties, hardships and dangers of all kinds; seldom without a Bowie knife or revolver, one was forced by circumstances to gain a lesson in self-reliance...
>
> Amongst numerous adventures, two will always be vividly remembered. One when the barn I was sleeping in was struck by lightning, and my bed was knocked to pieces underneath me, and I was myself stunned whilst the horse in the stable below was killed on the spot by the same stroke of lightning. We skinned the horse the same evening and for nights afterwards heard the wolves howling around its carcass.
>
> The second event was receiving a bullet wound in my leg and having to drive 12 miles to have it cut out, an operation which took at least an hour and without the comfort of chloroform.
>
> It was in these parts that one got a first experience in practical building, from log houses and barns, to a more respectable kind of brick and wooden house. It was here that I was initiated into the mysteries of door and window-sash making – rough, but strong and practical.

Seeing the uselessness of throwing my life away in these parts, and that few Englishmen succeeded in making more than a bare living, and yet not wishing to return home like a bad penny, I started for Canada, landing at St. Catherines in winter of 1872, but I could obtain no employment...

It was at this point that Fellowes Prynne first became actively involved in the world of architecture. His notes do not tell us whether he set out specifically to look for employment in this field, but they continue with his story:

... so I went on to Toronto, where I obtained temporary work in the office of an architect in the small way of business, but later on, through the introduction of the Rev. Darling upon whom I had called, I got a place of Junior Assistant in the office of one of the best known Toronto architects, R. C. Windyer, who was at the time carrying out new Custom House buildings for the government.

The terms of my employment were to work for what I was worth, and very little it must have been at the time, considering that my only credentials were my natural taste for drawing and my experience in the Wild West. But work I did for dear life…. With the kindness and sympathy that it would be hard to exaggerate, Mr. Windyer helped forward my studies giving me the use of his library and drawings….

By January 1875 I had gained a senior position in the office, and it was shortly after that my father received an offer from the late G. E. Street, R.A., to take me into his office.

I may here remark as a point of interest that my father gave Mr. Street his first church, [in Par, Cornwall] and that he (Mr. Street) had often expressed his gratitude to him for giving him this start, as the immediate outcome was 3 other churches in Cornwall.

On my return from America I worked in Mr. Street's office during 1875 and 1876, in after years, working with Swinfen Harris, R. J. Withers, A. Waterhouse R.A., and at the London School Board offices. I was a student at the Royal Academy 1876 and 77–78.

George Fellowes Prynne set up in his own practice in 1880 and Street was one of his sponsors for his ARIBA the following year. He stated that his first work 'of importance' was the completion in 1880–2 of his father's church, St Peter's in Plymouth (Fig. 2), the chancel of which had been built to Street's design in 1849–50.

George Fellowes Prynne's marriage to Bertha Geraldine Bradbury was registered in June 1882 in Wandsworth District. They were to have seven children, five boys and two girls. It is clear from my contact with his family, most notably his late daughter-in-law, Gwen Fellowes-Prynne (whose husband Aubrey had the hyphen officially inserted into their name to end confusion once and for all) that George Fellowes Prynne was a profoundly religious man with Anglo-Catholic convictions. Family prayers were said daily for the whole household. He was totally dedicated, not just to the use of his skills as an architect and

Fig. 2: Plymouth, St Peter. Interior as planned, looking east, from the Building News, *12 November 1880. G. E. Street's east end can be made out, as can Fellowes Prynne's idea to use this entirely as the sanctuary with the eastern bay of the nave being designated as the choir, as shown by the low screen and change of decoration in the ceiling.*

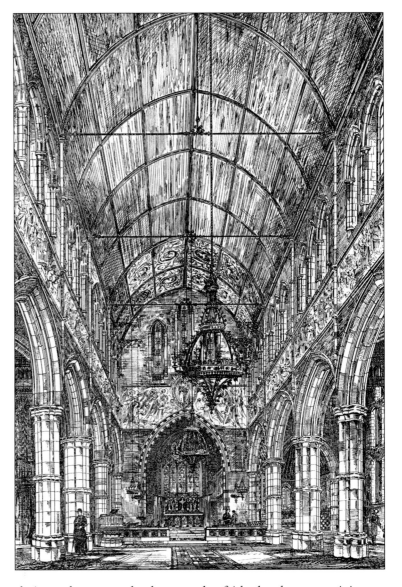

designer, but to apply them to the faith that he was striving to express.[2] Particularly in his latter years, he was heavily involved in the life of his parish in Ealing, being a sidesman at St Saviour's church (Fig. 3) of 1899 which he designed, but which is now sadly demolished following war damage.

After the consecration of St Peter's, Plymouth, in 1882, George Fellowes Prynne went on to design some two dozen new churches, including the large-scale incomplete church of All Saints, West Dulwich (1888–92, and now rebuilt after a major fire), and the Devon churches of St Peter at Budleigh Salterton (1891–3, Fig. 4), and St John the Baptist in Horrabridge (1892–3). In these three early works can be seen the full range of design features associated with the architect. All Saints was grand and

lofty, designed to seat 1,600 worshippers, but only four of the planned seven bays were completed. This brick-built church had a magnificent stone rood screen, destroyed in the fire, which was the first of many that were to become a feature of the architect's work. Fellowes Prynne is known to have given lectures on the subject of screens[3] and it is likely that he would have seen and been influenced by one or both of the great medieval Essex stone screens at Stebbing and Great Bardfield (Fig. 5).

St Peter, Budleigh Salterton, is of a scale more suited to a smaller town. Once again, it was never finished (the tower was never built) but it is typical of the architect's work in every way. It was described as 'a stately and beautiful building, worthy to rank among the finest modern churches in the country', with an 'extremely dignified' interior and the magnificence of the 'richly vested altar...contributing to the impressive appearance of this fine interior'.[4] St John the Baptist in Horrabridge is the nearest Fellowes Prynne came to designing a village church. The scale of the building is intimate, yet it bears most of the architect's hallmarks. Externally it bears less resemblance to a barn than many of the bigger buildings, being less lofty and having a large area of tiled roof. St Peter, Staines. Middlesex (1893–4, Fig. 7), was Fellowes Prynne's next work, and in many ways one of his greatest. Other examples are to be found at Weymouth, Dorset (St Paul, Westham, 1896, won in competition), Roehampton, Surrey (Holy Trinity, 1896–8), Sidcup, Kent (St John's, 1899–1902, Fig. 6),

Fig. 3: Ealing, St Saviour, London, 1899. This postcard, which predates September 1915, shows features typical of Fellowes Prynne's urban churches – polychrome stone and brickwork, a stone and marble pulpit, tiers of images of saints at the chancel arch, a low chancel screen wall, and a rich setting for the high altar. (Author's collection)

Fig. 4: Budleigh Salterton, St Peter, Devon, as illustrated in the Building News, *28 April 1893. The tower was never started.*

Fig. 5: Great Bardfield, St Mary the Virgin, Essex, and its medieval stone screen which is one of those thought to have inspired George Fellowes Prynne's own full-height stone screens. Historic postcard. (Author's collection)

Bognor Regis, West Sussex (St Wilfrid, 1905), Worcester (St Martin, 1911), and Taplow, Buckinghamshire (St Nicolas, 1912).

To illustrate Fellowes Prynne's approach to his work, I take two case studies, one a new church, St Peter, Staines; the other a major restoration, St Mary the Virgin, Payhembury in Devon, completed in 1897.

A new church – St Peter's, Staines, 1896–8

In the church of St Peter, Staines (Figs. 7 & 8), some 18 miles west of London, can be seen an example of Fellowes Prynne's work at its most successful. The site is perfect: an expanse of land in which the architect could express himself freely, with the added visual bonus of a riverside location. The building overlooks the Thames with no obstruction other than its own attractive lych-gate. Furthermore, the munificence of the benefactor, Sir Edward Clarke, Q.C., ensured that a building of the highest quality could be achieved, and St Peter's is one of the few churches completed almost exactly to Fellowes Prynne's original designs. He said of it that the building, its workmanship, sculpture or everything else connected with it gave him more satisfaction that had any other he had designed.

Fig. 6: Sidcup, St John, Kent, 1899–1901. The half-completed tower can be seen in this postcard sent in 1905. Compare this with Fig. 7 which shows a church where the tower was completed. (Author's collection)

The *Illustrated Church News* for 4 August 1894 gives the following account of the building, based on the architect's own description:[5]

> The style chosen in design is a free treatment of perpendicular in red brick and stone. The nave is of four bays, twenty six feet wide by eighty feet in length having a height of forty feet to the apex of the waggon roof. The chancel is of the same width and height as the nave. There is a narthex at the west end with western entrance. The tower, which is placed at the south-west end of the south aisle is designed in three stages, and capped with a copper covered spire. In the lower stage on the nave floor level a baptistry is formed.
>
> A southern transept with separate entrance forms the nave of a small chapel on the south side of the chancel. On the north side of the chancel are clergy and choir vestries with the organ choir.
>
> The altar is elevated by nine steps from the nave floor level, and ample space and height is left above and behind the altar for a baldechin or reredos. One of the main features of the church is the constructional rood screen, which is carried right up into the chancel arch, the portion of which is enriched with tracery. The central figure and rood are designed to be cut out of the solid stonework of the tracery, and the side figures placed on corbels formed in the panels of the tracery. This feature is quite unique, no other example of similar treatment existing. The furniture of the church is of an appropriate and ornate character. Choir stalls have been presented by Sir Edward, and the altar, which is of very elaborate design and highly decorated in gold colours, is a gift of Lady Clarke.

Externally the building is of red brick contrasted with white stonework, a use of materials typical of Fellowes Prynne. Gwen Fellowes-Prynne said that her father-in-law had a tremendous flair for colour and that he liked his work to be colourful amongst so many drab aspects of life. The church proclaims its existence boldly, particularly with the copper spire, weathered to the distinctive malachite green, atop. The tower in particular has

Fig. 7: Staines, St Peter, Middlesex, 1893–4, from a postcard predating 1930. This view of the building is little changed today. (Author's collection)

interesting detail. The lowest of the three stages has, above the baptistry door, representations of saints, including St Peter. This is not a common device in Fellowes Prynne's churches, but is effective and well-executed here. The second stage has lancet windows above the saints, with decorative relief above. The third stage houses a splendid peal of eight bells and, as well as the large louvred belfry windows, has the relief detail repeated, and an even smaller scale version of the same above that. This combination of figures, windows and texture, together with the decorative use of the stone, gives the tower a richness and attractiveness not bettered by the architect. Sadly, at so many of Fellowes Prynne's churches cost precluded the completion of the tower. St Peter's shows how integral the tower is to the overall design, and the building is so much better balanced for its presence. St John's church Sidcup (Fig. 6), with its incomplete tower, provides a comparison.

Inside, there is a great sense of space and height (Fig. 8). The dominant feature is the great stone screen, which became a hallmark of Fellowes Prynne's larger church designs such as at Holy Trinity, Roehampton (Fig. 9), and St Nicolas, Taplow among others. Another striking feature of the interior at St Peter's is the warmth of the colour. Here we have Fellowes Prynne's favoured red brick and white stone polychrome which works well in a building on this grand scale. The graceful piers and arches are simple and well proportioned. The radius of each arch is comfortable to the eye, and balanced in the context of the height and breadth of the nave. The arches are entirely stone-faced, whereas sometimes he favoured polychromatically treated stone and brick as was at St Saviour, Ealing (Fig. 3). The roof at Staines is typical of Fellowes Prynne with its barrel construction giving a

Fig. 8: Staines, St Peter, showing the stone rood screen on a postcard postmarked 1903. (Author's collection)

clean, smooth, appearance. In the clerestory, between each pair of windows, is a stone corbel column ending at the cusp between each nave arch with a carved angel. Side aisles give balance to the interior, and they are enhanced by some of the best stained glass in the church. There is no Lady Chapel as such which is unusual for Fellowes Prynne; the south transept is used for this purpose.

On the north side of the nave, close to the chancel steps, is a stunning wrought brass pulpit. This kind of pulpit can be seen in a number of Fellowes Prynne's churches, in particular, St Peter, Budleigh Salterton (Fig. 4). It has details around the base of the metal work showing fishes, and the letters 'S' and 'P'. The base is no less attractive with decorative stonework and coloured pillars. Behind the pulpit is the stone chancel wall, a feature found in almost all of the architect's complete churches and many of his restorations. From it springs the great stone screen, but there is also a wrought-iron and brass screen on the low stone wall at the entrance to the chancel. There are wrought-iron and brass gates to close off the chancel which, once again, are typical of the architect.

The chancel is wide, giving ample room for three rows of choir stalls on either side. These are of oak and are richly carved, as is the imposing organ case. The chancel is three steps higher than the nave, and a further six steps rise to the high altar. At the sanctuary there are wrought brass communion rails, and behind them the kind of colourful marble tiling favoured by the architect and others of his generation. Behind the altar is a coloured dossal curtain, and this was originally flanked by two more which have since been removed. It is possible that a reredos was originally intended, judging from evidence elsewhere.

The altar table itself is entirely typical of Fellowes Prynne's design. It is large, and designed for the frontal to be placed inside the structure, allowing the elaborate embroidery and appliqué to show through, framed by the three segments of the front of the altar. At Staines, there are frontals for the different seasons of the Church's year. At other locations, for example Holy Trinity, Roehampton, the architect's brother Edward painted panels to be on display permanently. The altar is stepped at the back, to allow for candlesticks, and there is a tabernacle over which the prominent cross is placed.

In the south-west corner of the church is the baptistry, located below the tower. The most striking feature here is the carved font cover with lavish tracery and pinnacles. This cover is not unlike others designed by Fellowes Prynne, such as at Holy Trinity, St Austell, but it is one of his best.

Fig. 9: Roehampton, Holy Trinity, Surrey, 1896–8. The stone screen on a postcard postmarked 1907. (Author's collection)

The congregation is provided with chairs, which Fellowes Prynne is on record as preferring over benches, believing them to be are more versatile and comfortable.[5] These are set on wooden parquet flooring; the aisles are of red tiles, with edging of cream and black. This arrangement of wood and tiles is to be found in almost all his churches, as are chairs wherever he could get his way.

St Peter's is fortunate in possessing a series of stained glass windows, all designed by the same artist, George's brother, Edward Arthur Fellowes Prynne (died 1921). These are of immense quality and beauty, and complement the rest of the interior perfectly. Edward Prynne is chiefly known for his religious artwork but was also a portrait painter. Edward's obituary in *The Builder* for 13 January 1922 says of him: 'After a preliminary study in art schools in London he went to Antwerp – studied under M. Verlat (whose influence is noticeable in his earlier work) and then to Florence, Rome and Paris. On his return he showed a preference for the Pre-Raphaelite school, which influenced the whole of his future work. In his views on art generally he was very single minded, and always aimed at seeing the good points in a fellow man's work, if such there were, rather than offer severe criticism.' Edward collaborated with his brother in several other projects, including the altar panels at Holy Trinity, Roehampton, and St Mary, East Grinstead, West Sussex, and reredoses at St Winifred's Manaton, Devon, and St John's, Penzance. It is worth quoting his obituary by Sir Edward Clarke, published in the St Peter's monthly magazine:

In Memoriam
GEORGE FELLOWES PRYNNE
All who are, or at any time have been, interested in our beautiful Church, will have heard with regret of the death of its gifted architect. George Prynne was the eldest son of the revered and beloved Father Prynne, who was for fifty years vicar of St. Peter's, Plymouth. For twenty of those years he was my kind and faithful friend, and when the time came for the division of the Parish of Staines, and the building of a new Church, it seemed natural that the name of St. Peter should be used here, and that the son of my old friend, who had already at Plymouth and at Budleigh Salterton shown a special capacity for ecclesiastical architecture, should be entrusted with the duty of designing the new building and superintending its erection.

He performed that most congenial task with a skill that amounted to genius, and an untiring diligence in supervising every detail of the work; even the dossal and frontal and the sanctuary kneelers and cushions were designed by him. And his success at Staines had not a little to do with him being afforded subsequent opportunities of showing his great qualities as an architect. At Roehampton and Dulwich and Bournemouth [St Alban's church] and Ealing there are notable examples of his skill, at Columb [sic] there is a partially erected cathedral, which if completed according to his designs, will be a notable example of the expression in architecture of religious devotion.

His life and work were cruelly shadowed by the great war. The building of beautiful churches appears for the time to have ceased. And two of his sons gave their lives for their country. Through it all he was a Christian gentleman; modest, kindly, diligent and patient. His brother, Edward, eminent in another form of devotional art, supplied the beautiful windows of our Church, and before his death, completed the designs for the windows still unfilled. And St. Peter's stands as a worthy monument to the two brothers.

May 1927 EDWARD CLARKE

A restored church: St Mary, Payhembury, 1894–7

By the end of the nineteenth century church restoration was generally usually very different from what it had been up to the 1870s. The battle against radical and gratuitous change had largely been won and architects like Fellowes Prynne generally subscribed to the principles that had been successfully enunciated by the Society for the Preservation of Ancient Buildings. There are apparent aberrations in Prynne's work but these are few and far between. His approach to restoration can be well illustrated by his work at the late medieval church at Payhembury in Devon, for which the report of his survey on 8 November 1894 survives.[6] This reveals his careful archaeological approach, and desire to undo the deterioration that had taken place and insensitive changes made during previous work. Extracts of this report now follow:

Generally
The church which is very picturesquely situated is of 15th century work, and has some very noteworthy points of interest. The general plan is similar to that of many Devon Churches i.e. a Nave and Chancel of nearly even width and height – a single Aisle on the North side with a Chapel at its East End, – a Tower at the West End of the nave and a Southern Porch...

Restoration
A Gallery of very unsightly proportions and design, supported on Iron columns, has been placed at the West End of the Church, entirely blocking up the Tower arch, and partially blocking one bay of the Nave Arcade...

Flooring
The flooring of the Church generally is in the form of stone slabs, laid on the natural ground without concrete under, wooden platforms being placed under the seats. The flooring is necessarily uneven, cold and damp.

Walling
The walling is generally in fair condition with the exception of part of the Southern Nave wall, which is bulging outwards. The original Rood loft staircase exists in the North wall but has been blocked up ...

The Arcade
There are five bays to the Arcade – four arches between the Nave, and one between the chancel and the North Aisle. The shafts, capitals, and bases of columns, and the Arches, are of Beer stone, and remain in

very fair condition, except where injured by the outward thrust of the Nave Roof.

The Roofs

The Roofs are of the usual Devon waggon type, – the original timbers and some of the original bosses at the intersection of ribs remain. The Roof timbers, however, are in very poor and rotten condition and a careful examination shows that the feet of rafters, and the wall plates, are in a state of advanced decay.

The Chancel Roof is at a lower level than the Nave Roof. The original pitch of the Chancel Roof has been altered, owing probably to the lower ends of the Rafters becoming rotten and being consequently cut off. The whole of the curved moulded ribs of this roof, are obliterated. The Roof Battens and slates are in very poor condition.

A Rough Brick Arch has been built between Chancel and Nave, evidently with the object of stopping the Western end of the lower Chancel Roof.

Fittings

The Church is rich in some of the remains of the furniture.

Rood Screen

The Rood Screen, as shown in the two photographs, [not available] is of great beauty, and although it has suffered considerably from decay, and other injury, it retains throughout its original lines, and rich detail, and can easily be restored to its original beauty.

Seats

The Central Block of Seats in the Nave are some of the original 15th Century seats with which the church was formerly seated throughout. The seats are massive, and have elaborately carved ends. In the other parts of the Nave, and in the North Aisle, they have unfortunately been replaced by ugly boxpew seats, which are as uncomfortable as they are unsuited to the Church. These modern seats have been crowded up against the Rood Screen in a manner that prevents all dignity of effect, and thus spoiling one of the most interesting & beautiful details in the Church.

The Pulpit

The base of the Pulpit shows that the present erection superseded an elaborately carved 17th century pulpit. The present late 18th century pulpit has been put up without any regard for the groined cornice of screen which has been hacked away to make room for the sounding board supports.

He then set out his proposals:

From the foregoing sketch of the present state of Peyhembury [sic] Church, it will be at once evident, that the timely restoration is of a great importance & interest to all who value the welfare of the Church, and who wish to see the beautiful works of art that it contains preserved from further decay.

Plans

In this report I enclose two plans – one showing the Church as at present, and one showing the proposed alteration as regards the plan.

The Scheme for restoration would, in the first place include to remove the present ugly gallery, at the West end of the Church, to form a proper Bell Ringers floor at about the same level as the present floor, but within the Tower, to open up the Tower arch entirely. To remove the seats at present placed against the screen, thus leaving a clear passage in front of, and opening up to view the entire screen. To put chairs in liew [sic] of the wretched little seats at present under the tower, to remove the present modern boxpews, and replace them by carved benches similar to those in the central position of the Church.

Within the Chancel the Clergyman's seat is simply altered for greater convenience. To restore the step in the Sanctuary to its original level, and the parclose screen between Chancel and Chapel to its original position.

To take up floor, laying cement concrete all over the surface of ground, and relaying paving in the Nave, Aisle and Porch, and putting tiles in the Chancel floor.

The general repair and repointing of the walls, externally, and replastering internally.

The repair of all defective stone dressings in Windows, and doorways, & arches etc.

The reglazing of Windows in the Nave & Aisle, re-using what is possible.

The entire renewal of the Nave and Chancel and South Porch roofs, and complete restoration of the Aisle Roof, reusing some of the ornamental work where good enough, and raising the Chancel roof to its original pitch.

To carefully restore and redecorate the Rood Screen.

To make externally some alterations in the Boundary Walls, and steps, so as to make them better, stronger, and more convenient.

The wall of church and Tower will be repointed.

The foregoing gives a general idea of the proposed restoration, but before giving more detailed particulars, beyond those indicated herein, and on the plans, it will be necessary for me to make very careful inspection of the more hidden parts, during the progress of the works, when some slight alterations may be found to be necessary, but in the main the restoration will be as herein described but whatever is found necessary will be done in the very best and most workmanlike manner.

In conclusion I can only say it will be my aim to keep and restore the old work as far as possible, and only to renew where absolutely necessary, that all the most noticeable, and interesting features may still be retained, which all interested, have been accustomed to associate with Peyhembury Church.

I am yours faithfully.

Geo: H. Fellowes Prynne Arch

This report provided the platform needed for discussion between the parish and the architect. What it demonstrates well are Fellowes Prynne's powers of observation and attention to detail, and, more importantly, his whole attitude to the business of restoration. The visitor to Payhembury church today will see a well-loved, well-cared-for church, with, among other things, a sumptuous chancel roof and a fully-restored and decorated rood screen (Figs. 10 & 11).

Fig. 10: Payhembury, St Mary, Devon, restored in 1895–7. Restoration of the rood screen and chancel roof were part of the works that followed on from Fellowes Prynne's report of 1894. (Author)

Final years

The First World War brought bitter blows for George Fellowes Prynne. Four of his five sons were in active service: Aubrey was blown over by a shell and his heart was displaced, and Harold was invalided out of the Army with severe dysentery. Both Aubrey and Harold recovered, but Aubrey never again enjoyed good health. Tragically, both Edgar and Norman Fellowes Prynne were killed in active service, Gwen Fellowes-Prynne commented that it was as if something within George Fellowes Prynne himself died with his sons.

After the war the opportunities for church architects were dramatically reduced and for a number of years were largely confined to the commemoration of the fallen. War memorials, therefore, whether in the form of a chapel, the erection of a cross, a wall-tablet, a screen or other items of church furnishings, form

Fig. 11: Payhembury St Mary, looking east. (Author)

the bulk of Fellowes Prynne's output into the early 1920s. Otherwise there were various items of furniture or decorations for chancels.

The one fairly large job which was started in this time, the enlargement of the south aisle and chancel of St John, Farnham Common in Buckinghamshire, begun in 1924, was never completed in his lifetime, and was abandoned midway through construction after his death, which occurred on 7 May 1927. His last work to be completed in his lifetime was the memorial reredos at the church of the Holy Cross in Crediton, Devon (Fig. 12).

In all, George Fellowes Prynne is known to have had a hand in the building or restoration of almost 200 churches. For more on George Fellowes Prynne and a catalogue of his work, please go to www.gfp.sharville.org.uk The author is aware that there are at time of writing some inaccuracies to remedy, and would welcome any additions to this list and any further corrections that need to be made.

Fig. 12: Crediton, Holy Cross, Devon. The reredos was the last of Fellowes Prynne's works completed in his lifetime and was dedicated in the year of his death, 1927. (Author)

Acknowledgements

I could not have prepared this piece without the help of three special people. Firstly, the Revd Selwyn Tillett who researched the architect with me and opened up a new world of record offices and archives to me. Secondly, the late Gwen Fellowes-Prynne, who graciously agreed to talk freely into a cassette recorder microphone about her father-in-law. Thirdly I must thank Gwen's son – George's grandson – J. Rundle Fellowes-Prynne, for the loan of family documents and photos, and his unstinting encouragement over the many years I have been working on this project.

Notes

1 A copy of these manuscript notes is held by the author courtesy of Mr Rundle Fellowes-Prynne.
2 Transcript of taped interview between the author and the late Gwen Fellowes-Prynne on 1 June 1985.
3 For example a lecture to Devon and Exeter Architectural Society as reported in *The Builder*, 27 Feb 1897.
4 *The Church in the West*, 29 April 1893.
5 Letter to the Revd F. E. Coope of Thurlestone, 23 March 1904. Copy held by author courtesy of Mr Rundle Fellowes-Prynne.
6 Copy of manuscript report from Devon Record Office, DRO2974A/PI1.

The ecclesiastical work of Hugh Thackeray Turner

Robin Stannard

THE ARTS AND CRAFTS architect Hugh Thackeray Turner (1853–1937: Fig. 1) is best known as the influential secretary of the Society for the Protection of Ancient Buildings (SPAB), a position he held for 29 years between 1882 and 1911. He was a pupil of Sir George Gilbert Scott and became the chief assistant to his son, George Gilbert junior. In 1885 he entered into partnership with Eustace Balfour, forming the practice of Balfour Turner which was mainly involved in residential work, particularly on the Grosvenor Estate in Mayfair where it is credited with introducing the principles of the Arts and Crafts Movement into the heart of London. Turner's best-known building is Westbrook, his own house at Godalming, built in 1900, an outstanding example of Arts and Crafts house and garden design, which Pevsner compared favourably to contemporary work by Lutyens and Voysey.[1] Pevsner was also lavish in his praise of another building by Turner in west Surrey – the Wycliffe Building, Guildford, which he designed in 1892 for his father-in-law, the wealthy stockbroker, Thomas Wilde Powell. It was an experiment in working-class housing which Pevsner described as 'up to the best English (hence, at this time, European) work of the nineties.'[2]

Robin Stannard is a historic building surveyor who works for the architectural practice, Scott Brownrigg. He began his conservation career with the SPAB architect David Nye, and then went on to work for English Heritage. He has a special interest in the Arts and Crafts Movement and has spent several years researching the life and work of Hugh Thackeray Turner.

Fig. 1: Thackeray Turner, 1886, aged 33, the same year as he was elected a member of the Art Workers' Guild. (Art Workers' Guild)

This chapter, however, concentrates on Thackeray Turner's ecclesiastical work which falls into three main areas: his early career with the Scotts; his efforts, as secretary of the SPAB, to promote sensitive church restorations; and his two remarkable new churches, St Anselm, Mayfair (1893–6) and Crown Court Church, Convent Garden (1905–9) which reveal an architect who did not conform to contemporary ideas of church design and rebelled against the very principles of the Victorian Gothic Revival.

Early life and character

Hugh Thackeray Turner was born in 1853, at Foxearth, Essex, the son of a country vicar, the Revd John Turner. The family were well off and very artistic. Thackeray Turner was one of five sons and two daughters. His elder brother Hawes became a painter and later the keeper and secretary of the National Gallery, London. Thackeray Turner's younger brother, Laurence (1864–1957), trained as an architect but developed a successful career as a carver who often collaborated with his brother. Laurence also undertook commissions for many leading architects including Bodley, Sir Herbert Baker, William Weir, Henry Hare, Sir Walter Tapper, and Curtis Green. He taught a number of Arts and Crafts craftsmen including George Jack, and played a leading role in the renaissance of English carving.

Through the influence of his family, Thackeray Turner developed a keen sense of social duty, an appreciation of art and music, a love of the countryside, antiquarian interests, enjoyment of sport, but most significantly, a deep conviction in the importance of honesty and integrity in life – something that had impact upon his architectural work. He was a meticulous man who was characterised by *The Survey of London* as 'reticent and modest.'[3] Yet he enjoyed the company of others and had many friends and acquaintances within the liberal-thinking, social-reforming areas of society. F. W. Troup in 1938 described him as follows:

> I first met Turner many years ago as a member of the Art Workers' Guild. Here he was a frequent speaker. His comments were always vigorous and to the point. He said what he thought and never lost his temper. He expected his opponents and often succeeded in getting them to reply in the same manner, and he seemed to enjoy controversy about any matter he was interested in. But it was at the executive committee of the SPAB, that I got to know Turner intimately and learned to admire his fighting qualities, which I fear made him not a few enemies in his robust eagerness to save ancient buildings from disfiguration or vandalism.[4]

Education and work for Sir George Gilbert Scott

Thackeray Turner's brothers, Laurence and Hawes both attended Marlborough College and went on to Oxford and Cambridge respectively. By contrast, Turner was educated at Newbury Grammar School and then went to work as an assistant to an unknown architect in London. In 1874, aged 21, he was articled to Sir Gilbert Scott who was then nearing the end of his long, successful career. Gavin Stamp, describes his office, as 'developing into the prototype of the modern large architectural firm producing a consistent house style.'[5] Little is known of Turner's work for Scott but during his time there he made many contacts that would prove significant to his future career. However, like some other architects who trained under the leading architects of the Gothic Revival, Turner rebelled against the style. Troup's appreciation of him states that from his experience in the office 'he learned much to be avoided, and acquired an almost instinctive revulsion of the Gothic Revival, whether for church or any other form of building.'[6]

Scott felt that restoration was causing great damage to medieval churches and had in 1864 been involved in the foundation of the RIBA Committee on the Conservation of Ancient Architectural and Monuments Remains. Yet he himself was accused of carrying out conjectural restorations and, as President of the RIBA, was singled out as a target by the conservation movement. In 1877 William Morris founded the Society for the Protection of Ancient Buildings and began to publicly criticise Scott and his approach to church restoration. Turner would surely have been well aware of the controversy thus created.

Work for George Gilbert Scott junior

After Sir Gilbert Scott died in 1878 Thackeray Turner continued to work for the office under Scott's son, John Oldrid. It seems this change did not suit him because seven months later he left to become George Gilbert Scott junior's chief assistant.[7] Scott junior was then aged 39 and at the height of his brilliant, but tragically brief career, cut short by mental illness. This new opportunity must have been very appealing for the 25-year-old Turner since Scott was a leading figure in the development of church design and an important figure in the Queen Anne Revival.

Scott's other assistant at this time was Temple Lushington Moore who had joined him as an articled pupil in 1875. On completing his articles, Moore continued working in close collaboration with Scott, remaining a loyal friend and eventually building up his own successful architectural practice. Moore would become one of the leading late Gothic Revival church architects, carrying forward on the path set by Scott junior.[8]

Little is known of Turner's work for Scott junior, but as the latter's mental condition began to decline, he became increasingly dependent on his two principal assistants to manage the day-to-day running of the practice. During the five years that Turner worked for the younger Scott the office was involved in a wide variety of important projects, including the new church of All Hallows, Southwark, ongoing work at St Agnes', Kennington, new residential buildings at Pembroke College, Cambridge, and St John's College, Oxford.[9]

The office was also heavily involved in church repairs and alterations. Scott junior was generally more aware of the need to conserve historic buildings than his father. This is demonstrated by his campaign to preserve the tower of Hampstead parish church during the 1870s and the sensitive repair and alteration work which he carried out at Pembroke College, Cambridge (1878–82), the latter being undertaken while Turner was employed by him. Scott was generally sympathetic to the SPAB and knew many of those involved in the formation of the society, although he did not agree with all its aims and did not become a member himself.[10]

However, the SPAB did not trust Scott to always show restraint in his church restorations. Such wariness was justified by what happened at St Andrew's, Cherry Hinton in Cambridgeshire, where he reassured J. J. Stevenson, acting for the SPAB, that, 'he was very desirous of promoting the conservation of the old building.'[11] In the end he carried out very extensive work to the church, including rebuilding the walls of the nave and chancel, putting on a new nave roof and virtually renewing that on the chancel. This all took place between 1878 and 1880, when Turner was employed by Scott although it is not known whether he played any role in the project. One significant aspect of this scheme was that the SPAB were alerted to potential danger by Turner's future partner, Eustace Balfour, then studying at Cambridge. Balfour, whilst still a student, became an early member of the SPAB, and afterwards a pupil of the Queen Anne Revival architect, Basil Champneys.

If there is uncertainty about his role at Cherry Hinton church, then it is evident from correspondence in the SPAB archive, that Turner played an important part in the repairs by Scott to the church of St Peter & St Paul, Knapton in Norfolk. The church is famous for its double hammerbeam roof, decorated by three tiers of angels holding shields. This roof was in very poor condition and it was proposed to remove it. Protests by the SPAB to the Master of Peterhouse resulted in Scott junior being appointed. Unlike Cherry Hinton church, Scott went to great lengths to preserve the character of the building, even retaining, where possible, the external plaster.[12]

George Wardle for the SPAB kept a close watch on the work, whilst Turner handled the correspondence for Scott. Wardle and J. Henry Middleton (a friend of Turner's) inspected the church and reported in the 1882 SPAB annual report that 'A letter was addressed to Mr. Scott by the Committee, explaining their views on what ought to be done, which Mr. Scott received with a very friendly spirit, expressing his agreement with views of the society in this instance'.[13] The SPAB wished 'strongly to protest against any attempt to replace the missing carved angels and other ornamental parts of the internal woodwork ... both from the feeling that modern copies of old carvings are feeble and spineless and also from the fear that it would pave the way towards a complete "Restoration" or repainting of all the coloured decoration – a process that would be equivalent to its total destruction.'[14]

The repairs at Knapton were generally considered to be an excellent example of the new conservative in restoration, although Scott chose to ignore the final piece of advice from the SPAB and replaced the missing carved angels with modern copies. However, he differentiated them by leaving the original carvings unpainted.

Work for the SPAB

It is likely that the success of the Knapton restoration that drew Thackeray Turner to the attention of the SPAB with the result that on the 13 December 1882 he was appointed as its paid, part-time secretary, aged 29.[15] This would be the turning point in his career. The move also spared him suffering the distress of Scott junior's mental decline which led to him being detained in the Royal Bethlem Hospital in 1883. From then onwards fluctuations between bouts of sanity and insanity made it increasingly difficult for him to practise.[16]

Turner's appointment as secretary of the SPAB would prove important to the future of the society, his character, experience and methodical nature making him the perfect person for the job. Chris Miele summed this up as follows:

> After its founding, the single most important moment for the Society in the early heroic period was in January 1883, when the young architect, Hugh Thackeray Turner, took up the post of part-time paid secretary. After Morris it was Turner who was most responsible for ensuring the future health of the Society. He seems to be enormously competent and efficient and his letters are small masterpieces of tact

and diplomacy though he could when required deploy the bitter irony biting invective that was Morris's real strength: it had become something of a house style.[17]

The SPAB's initial success as a protest group had been heavily reliant on William Morris's flare for publicity. As time went by it became increasingly apparent that the society needed to place itself on a firmer professional footing, and it is interesting to read Turner's own account (although written in the third person) of his appointment given at a SPAB annual meeting, 45 years later in 1927:

> If the 1880, 1881, and 1882 reports are read, the impression will be left that the work of the Society was very much a work of opposition, and it seems probable that this was due to the lay Secretaries being unable through want of technical knowledge, to explain fully how the Society wished the actual work of repairing carried out.

> The two architects who were Hon. Secretaries probably saw that if architects were to be imbued with the principles of the Society, it needed an architect to speak and write to them. At any rate, as a matter of fact, the 1883 Report bears the name of Thackeray Turner, who was an architect. It will be seen that from reading the Annual Reports that the strong opposition to the Society from the clergy and architects slowly died down. William Morris's dictum that we should 'mend' and not 'renew' slowly began to be accepted. It became clear to the Committee that if a 'restoration' was in contemplation it could not criticise the proposed work until it had in its hands a report on the building made by an architect who understood the Society's views. As the Secretary was an architect the Committee could send him to report on any building.[18]

Thackeray Turner's appointment was part-time with him working three days a week for the SPAB and thus enabling him to continue with his private practice. This latter work, the society suggested, should be conducted from its own offices, and this would lead to an association between the practice Balfour Turner and the SPAB, that would last until 1925. The association would then be continued until 1936, after the practice was renamed Powys MacGregor. Not surprisingly, Turner was prohibited from accepting architectural appointment for repair work to buildings in which the society was involved. As William Morris increasingly became involved in other interests, the running the SPAB passed to Turner and Philip Webb. The majority of its cases at this time concerned churches and Thackeray Turner fully endorsed and promoted William Morris's approach in matters of restoration.

An early case published in the 1886 *SPAB Annual Review* illustrates Turner's style of correspondence. This was influenced by Philip Webb and was diplomatic but biting, with an underlining dry ironic wit, borne out of disbelief of others' ignorance towards church conservation.[19] The correspondence relates to the church at Saltfleetby St Clement in Lincolnshire, which Turner sarcastically describes in the report as 'a not unfair example of opinion which passes for intelligence on this subject of the preservation of ancient art.' He originally wrote to the church on 10 July 1885 after the SPAB had learnt that a new building, in a different location, was proposed. He enquired what new use would be found for the old one. The reply, from an unknown correspondent the next day, offered the gratifying reassurance to the society that 'You may rest assured that I am too good an antiquarian to destroy anything worth retaining.' However, it then goes on to describe the intention to quite simply pull down the old church and use the materials to build part of their new one:

> It is intended faithfully to reproduce the old church on a new site, restoring the chancel (which was a Georgian thing built de nov about fifty years, minus the lead) to its original height and length, and restoring the tower to what we believe would be the original proportions, and building in stone instead of brick (the tower which I have pulled down was a pile of bricks and road scrapings with three little square windows in the belfry, with a lintel of rotten wood). Nearly every trace of the of the original Church (circs 1125) had disappeared, excepting a sweetly beautiful arcade separating the north aisle from the nave; and this bit of graceful and original work will be faithfully reproduced, stone buy stone, most carefully − every stone marked to come into its own place again, and not a morsel to be destroyed or injured, all tool marks to be carefully preserve

Thackeray Turner's blunt reply on 17 July was:

> I laid your letter of the 11th inst before the Committee of this Society at its last meeting, and I was directed to thank you for your kindness in replying to our inquiry, and to say that the Committee deeply grieves to hear that you have destroyed the old church, which obviously cannot be restored; that is, the new church will be of no historical interest, and almost worthless as a specimen of mediaeval art.

Turner expressed his thoughts on restoration in a long address to the society's annual meeting in 1896 which he used to criticise the clergy and architects who persisted in carrying out church restorations.[20] Firstly he describes the importance of ancient churches:

> It is no exaggeration to say that our ancient churches are the most important works of English art now existing. Built at a time when religious fervour was intense, and when architecture as an art, was at its highest level, this fervour and this art bestowed themselves upon these churches, and they have come down to us enriched with the added interest of centuries of historic associations.

He then describes how later periods of architecture in particular were destroyed by the cult of restoration:

in the first years of restoration, so much perpendicular work was ruthlessly destroyed by those whose sympathies were more with the earlier periods of gothic art, and so much valuable seventeenth and eighteenth century work has been more recently swept away; and now, just when we begin to feel how great these sacrifices were, we find they were made in vain, and that in seeking to go back to what was, the substance has been exchanged for the shadow … The result has been disastrous in the extreme; so sad has been the outcome of a rash impetuosity, that three-fourths of the remains of Ancient Buildings have been disfigured discredited beyond recognition.

Turner is critical of the attitude of many of the clergy to ancient buildings:

In knowing nothing that reminds me more (speaking ecclesiologically) of the desert strewn with the bones of what were once living and beautiful creatures, scraped of every particle of flesh, the marrow picked out of their bones, the soul, the divine spark of beauty and life expelled for ever. No sooner does a zealous incumbent find himself in the way of collecting money to his church, then he rubs his hands, and says embowelled will I see thee by and by. Falstaff was fortunately able to get away from the knife. Alas ! not so our beautiful old church. The architect and contractor are called in, and the embowelling goes on a pace. All the old fittings are cast forth, the walls are scraped and painted, and plaster is everywhere peeled off just as the skin was taken of St Bartholomew.

He described the work of some architects:

the architect is placed in an entirely false position in being called upon to determine what constitutes the interest of a church, and what features are, and are not, worthy of preservation.
His studies may have led him to an undue appreciation of one particular style and a corresponding neglect of others, or may cause him to regard ancient works merely as specimens, valuable only in proportion to their rareness; and he may be quite oblivious to their higher value, both as works of art and channels of human sympathy, bringing us in touch with our past generations of fellow men.
A far juster estimate is frequently formed by those who have worshipped in the church since their youth; but these are often deterred by their want of archaeological knowledge from opposing their sentiment to be over-awed by learning which really does not affect the question. It needs no special training to understand whether the architects plans aim at preservation or alteration. This is a simple matter of fact; and what is to be decided is, Shall the old church be maintained, or shall we have an archaeological exercise by the architect?

Turner is very critical of church architects:

Unfortunately, however, through the enchanting study of the mediaeval styles in building has led to a class of designers to supply an artificial demand, who have produced a semblance of the revival of the arts, which has deceived a majority of the people, yet these mere paper-scheming architects have mostly proved incompetent builders, and in repairing, altering and adapting the works of men who understood perfectly the allied crafts of the art, have shown little knowledge of the real foundations design.

The presence of Philip Webb and his promotion of conservation at the SPAB acted as a magnet for many innovating young Arts and Crafts architects, such as William Lethaby, Ernest Gimson, Sidney Barnsley, Alfred Powell, Detmar Blow, Frank Troup, William Weir, Henry Wilson and Charles Winmill. As Lethaby explained: 'What drew these young architects to the Society was Philip Webb, and the wish to pursue architecture as a craft, not only designing, but also taking an active part in the construction. The Society's emphasis on buildings in the country, had a parallel with these young designers interests in vernacular buildings and traditional rural crafts.'[21] With the encouragement of Philip Webb and Turner, some of these young architects began undertaking restoration work, which involved living on site, giving direct instruction to the workmen and physically undertaking conservation work. Turner in 1896 notes: 'A far nobler field lies open to our architects in repairing and upholding (instead of restoring) our churches. All their skill and ingenuity will come to play in underpinning walls, securing foundations, repairing roofs, removing the cause of damp, and upholding parts ready to fall.'[22]

Working in this manner, and directed by Webb in London, they developed innovative conservation techniques which proved that it was often possible to save buildings which might otherwise be demolished. Early examples include the tower to East Knoyle church, Wiltshire, and the tower to Clare, Suffolk, repaired by Detmar Blow in 1892 and 1898 respectively.[23] Turner was heavily involved in organising these dedicated, energetic, but sometimes disorganised young architects. In 1898, for example, he had to write in reprimand Detmar Blow regarding his lack of attendance on site at Clare church.[24]

In 1903, the SPAB published *Notes on the Repair of Ancient Buildings* (Figs. 2 & 3), a landmark book thought to have largely been written by Turner, although he did not claim credit for it. This may be partly because of his own modesty and partly because the book summarised the techniques developed by Philip Webb, working with Delmar Blow, Alfred Powell and William Weir over the previous ten years.

NEW BRICKWORK IN MAKING GOOD, CRACKS THROUGH THICKNESS OF WALL

BRICK LINTEL INSERTED THROUGH THICKNESS OF WALL

TEMPORARY WOOD CENTRE UNDER ARCH DURING REPAIRS TO WALL

PROPS.   PROPS.

FLOOR OF CHURCH

SECTION THROUGH CHANCEL SHEWING WALL OVER ARCH STRENGTHENED AND REPAIRED.

SCALE OF FEET.

Fig. 2: An illustration from the SPAB book, Notes on the Repair of Ancient Buildings *(1903). Thackeray Turner is considered to have largely written the book. It summarises the conservation work carried out Philip Webb and other SPAB architects. The illustrations were by William Weir. (SPAB)*

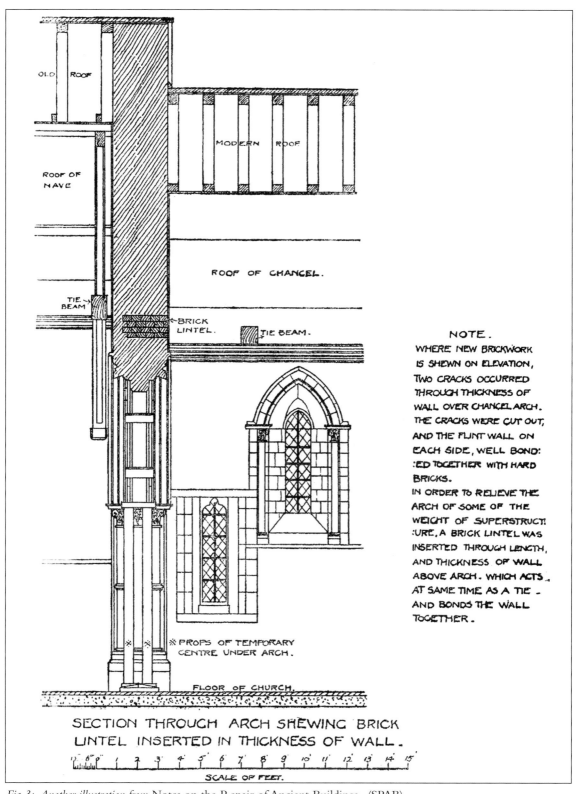

OLD. ROOF

MODERN ROOF

ROOF OF NAVE

ROOF OF CHANCEL.

TIE BEAM

BRICK LINTEL.

TIE BEAM.

NOTE.
WHERE NEW BRICKWORK
IS SHEWN ON ELEVATION,
TWO CRACKS OCCURRED
THROUGH THICKNESS OF
WALL OVER CHANCEL ARCH.
THE CRACKS WERE CUT OUT,
AND THE FLINT WALL ON
EACH SIDE, WELL BOND-
-ED TOGETHER WITH HARD
BRICKS.
IN ORDER TO RELIEVE THE
ARCH OF SOME OF THE
WEIGHT OF SUPERSTRUCT-
-URE, A BRICK LINTEL WAS
INSERTED THROUGH LENGTH,
AND THICKNESS OF WALL
ABOVE ARCH. WHICH ACTS
AT SAME TIME AS A TIE
AND BONDS THE WALL
TOGETHER.

* PROPS OF TEMPORARY
CENTRE UNDER ARCH.

FLOOR OF CHURCH.

SECTION THROUGH ARCH SHEWING BRICK
LINTEL INSERTED IN THICKNESS OF WALL.

SCALE OF FEET.

Fig 3: Another illustration from Notes on the Repair of Ancient Buildings. (SPAB)

The established architect

Thackeray Turner's appointment as secretary of the SPAB helped to introduce him to some of the most important figures in the Arts and Crafts movement. These connections were further increased by his election in 1886 as a member of the Art Workers' Guild. It is probably through the SPAB that he met the wealthy stockbroker Thomas Wilde Powell, a philanthropist, patron of the Arts and Crafts Movement, and an early SPAB member.[25] In 1888 Turner married Powell's daughter, Mary. This effectively guaranteed his future financial security, eventually allowing him to build his own house, Westbrook. Mary was herself involved in the Arts and Crafts Movement, exhibiting embroidery at the Arts and Crafts Society's exhibitions along with Turner's painted ceramic work. In 1907 she co-founded the Women's Guild of Arts with May Morris.[26]

It was also through the SPAB that Turner met the young Queen Anne Revival architect Eustace Balfour, who was acting as its honorary secretary. He was the youngest son of James Maitland Balfour of Whittingham, East Lothian, and his mother was Lady Blanche Cecil. His brother, Arthur, was to be a future prime minister and his sister was the principal of Newnham College, Cambridge.[2]

After graduating Balfour joined. Basil Champneys as a "'student' for the ordinary forms of pupilage were waived, and after a much shorter term of practical experience than is usually advised to a young Architect, he began to practice on his own account, and set forth on his career as an Architect.'[28] His first major architectural commission was the rebuilding of Ampton Hall in Suffolk which led him to take Thackeray Turner into partnership in 1885 thanks to the latter's greater experience in respect of such a complex project. The result, the *Builders' Journal & Architectural Record* noted, 'does not reproduce that which it succeeds, although, as will be noticed, the detail is in the tradition of the Jacobean period.'[29] This building set the architectural approach for much of the partnership's subsequent work, their designs being inspired by, but not directly copying, historic styles.

The partnership was not successful in securing further major architectural commissions until 1890 when Eustace Balfour was appointed surveyor to the Grosvenor Estate as a direct a result of Balfour's wife being the niece of the duke of Westminster. This gave the partners the opportunity of designing numerous buildings in Mayfair, including their first church.[30]

St Anselm, Mayfair

St Anselm, Davies Street, Mayfair (1893–6: Figs. 4–9) was the only Anglican church by Balfour Turner. It is one of only two churches designed by the practice, both of them generally considered to be the work of Turner. Closed in 1938 and then demolished, it was a very unusual design. It is contemporary with Thackeray Turner's Wycliffe Building in Guildford of 1892, an outstanding example of Arts and Crafts restraint and rational design. St Anselm's is rooted in Thackeray Turner's fundamental belief in architectural honesty, and his intention was 'to avoid introducing features … which call up remembrances of ancient buildings … as our present conditions of building render competition with such buildings impossible.'[31]

It combined a fourteenth-century Gothic exterior with a fourteenth-century classical Italian interior. Yet neither of these elements is a direct copy. Troup, writing in 1938, stated: 'In features and details there is little to suggest copying or following any phase of medieval architecture, except possibly the reticulated tracery of the windows.'[32] This collision of styles shows Webb's influence and would be used again by Turner for several secular buildings such as Lygon Place, London (1900) and Goodwynds Place, Dorking (1901). Their contrasting features were juxtaposed to create an impression of buildings which had evolved haphazardly over time. An influence on Turner was, no doubt, the historic buildings he was inspecting for the SPAB in which architectural features of different periods coexisted. It was the earlier Victorians' insistence on tidying up such inconsistencies, particularly in medieval churches, which the SPAB had fought so hard to resist.

The commission originated in the proposed demolition of the Hanover Chapel, Regent Street, a Commissioners' church of 1824–5 by C. R. Cockerell. By 1881 this had fallen on hard times and the Grosvenor Estate decided to demolish it and build a new church in Davies Street. It was not until 1890 that this plan came to fruition and 1893 before Balfour Turner were commissioned for the new church.[33] The proposed demolition of the Hanover Chapel met some opposition, principally from the RIBA which, 'objected to the demolition of one of London's very few monuments to Cockerell's refined and cultured taste.'[34] Given both Balfour and Turner's involvement with the SPAB, they remained curiously silent on the matter!

The design incorporated a new rectory, linked at high level to the church by a blind and pierced arcade, a device Turner used

Fig. 4: North-east view of St Anselm's, Mayfair, from Davies Street. The photograph was taken in 1937, shortly before the church was demolished. (Survey of London, 1980)

Fig. 5: North-west view of St Anselm's, from Weighhouse Street, 1937. (Survey of London, 1980)

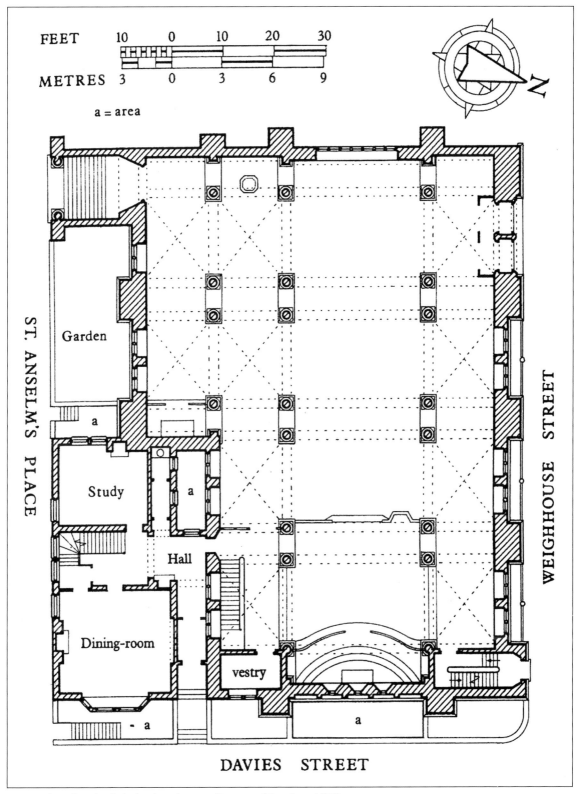

Fig. 6: Plan of St Anselm's church and rectory. (Survey of London, 1980)

Fig. 7: East elevation, St Anselm's church and rectory. (Survey of London, 1980)

later for the Philips Memorial, Godalming in 1912. Externally, the church comprises a steeply pitched tiled roof, double aisles, clerestory, prominent buttressing, and walls constructed of stock brickwork with Portland stone dressings. The austerity of the brickwork contrasts with the flamboyance of the sweeping curve to the paired buttresses which terminate in arched openings with protruding rainwater spouts. The most prominent decorative feature of the exterior are the reticulated tracery windows.

In contrast to the Gothic-inspired exterior, the interior is a surprise – spacious and light – with an overtly fourteenth-century Italian Renaissance flavour. *The Survey of London* compared it to 'church interiors of the of the Florentine quatrocento, especially to Brunelleschi's Santo Spirito and Pazzi Chapel. Not only the mouldings but the elliptical arches but also the alternating texture of light and shade breathed the spirit of the early Italian Renaissance.'[35]

The Survey of London and the Builders' Journal and Architectural Record both contain detailed descriptions on which the following is based.[36] The chancel and nave were undivided and between the nave arcades had paired columns in blue-grey Robin Hood stone from the Forest of Dean. The capitals were carved by Turner's brother Laurence. From the clerestory sprang paired arches with Robin Hood stone, these dividing the flat ceiling which was finished in dark Oregon pine. The aisles were rib-vaulted, as was the two-bay morning chapel next to the southwest entrance. The east wall of the chancel had of stone pilasters and arches with three small lancet windows with stained glass above which were representations of the Evangelists carved by Laurence Turner.

The staircase and vestry in the south-east corner of the church were divided from the main church by a pierced oak screen also by Laurence Turner. The *Builders' Journal & Architectural Record* said it 'is also a happy departure from the stereotyped Gothic forms … The panels are of open carved oak fret, representing the conventional vine, with grape clusters and birds, lilies, and the cresting is a continuous design of the same character.'

The choir was divided from the nave by a dwarf screen of Irish green marble topped with gunmetal or bronze and the choir demarcated a curved brass rail. The oak choir stalls were left with their chisel marks showing. In a similar way the design of the iron rails adjacent to the south porch and studding to the oak door clearly shows that they were crafted by a blacksmith.

Fig. 8: North elevation, St Anselm's church. (Survey of London, 1980)

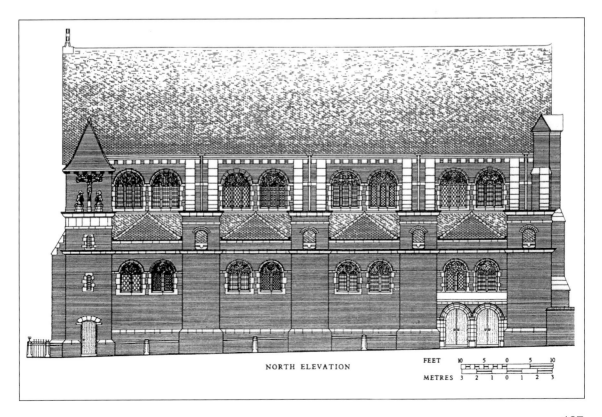

NORTH ELEVATION

FEET   10   5   0   5   10
METRES 3   2   1   0   1   2   3

Fig. 9: Interior of St Anselm's church in 1937. It features stone and timber carving by Thackeray Turner's brother, Laurence. (Survey of London, 1980)

The floor finish progressed from two tones of wood blocks in the side chapels to squares of Irish green, black and Pavonazzo marble in the sanctuary. In the spirit of the Arts and Crafts Movement, stone throughout the building was left with the tool marks showing. Similarly, the walls were finished in a single coat of plaster from the trowel and then whitewashed. At dado level the walls were finished in Powell opalescent glass tiles. All the windows were glazed with thick panes of Prior's glass made by Britten and Gibson and bound with saddles of gunmetal. The font was located at the west end of the south aisle and was octagonal in plan and made in black Alloa marble. There were future plans to cover the east wall in mosaic and to introduce additional colour into the church, but this did not materialise. In 1919, however, an oak pulpit was added, possibly by Laurence Turner.

The *Builders' Journal & Architectural Record* was very complimentary, describing the building as 'not only one of the most interesting of modern churches; but the best Church raised in London of late years.' Of the interior it enthused:

> The whole church is a very happy conception it catches a distant atmosphere of the severity Archaic without forcing a comparison with our present fashions; and it certainly shows how some such style as is amenable to the needs of modern church-goers, than the incompatible mysticism of the Gothic styles.
>
> There is none of the effort in straining traditional Gothic forms to new needs, which mars and destroys the homogeneity of John Sedding's Church [Holy Trinity, Sloane Street].[37]

This opinion, however, was not shared by others. Beresford Pite, fulminating in *Architectural Association Notes*, considered the church to be 'an insult both to Cockerell's Hanover Chapel and to the gentle memory of St Anselm's, and an exhibition of that pride of bastardy which is so prized today.'[38] Indeed, it would appear the church was not universally popular and, with a declining local population, in 1937 the Church Commissioners decided to pull it down. Turner's close friend F. W. Troup, unsuccessfully campaigned for the church to be re-erected on a suburban site but attracted little support from fellow architects, H. S. Goodhart-Rendel stating that the church was 'purely a personal record of Turner's personal tastes', and went on the to remark 'though I admit that its design has much historical significance as a revolt from Gothic in a fashionable neighbourhood, I feel that the building deprived of its context, historically and local, might be more of a curiosity than a thing of beauty.'[39]

Although Troup failed in his endeavour, he was successful attracting interest in elements of the church being used in a new building. The architect N. Cachemaille-Day had been associated with the building and stated that he was 'ready to build the successor church in the same spirit and tradition of architecture.' The new St Anselm's, was built at Belmont, Stanmore, using materials, many of the furnishings, and the Prior's glass from the old building.[40]

St Anselm's was controversial in its time. But, had it survived, with our broader understanding of the Arts and Crafts Movement, it would be greatly admired for its integrity and courage to break away from conventional church design of the period.

Crown Court Church

Balfour Turner's second church was the Crown Court Church, Covent Garden (Figs. 10–13), built for the Church of Scotland between 1906 and 1909. Ten years had elapsed since St Anselm's during which time Thackeray Turner had designed his most important building, his own house, Westbrook at Godalming. In 1905 he was elected as a fellow of the RIBA suggesting that, that after many years' distrust, he had concluded that the RIBA and SPAB held similar views on building conservation.

It was also a period of change and personal tragedy. William Morris had died in 1896 and in 1900 Philip Webb retired from architectural practice. Then in 1907 Turner's father died as did his wife, brought down by pneumonia, so leaving him to bring up three teenage daughters. Furthermore Eustace Balfour, now

Fig. 10: Main entrance to Crown Court Church from Russell Street. (Author)

Fig. 11: Crown Court Church from Crown Court. A school and hall were located at ground level, whilst the church occupied the upper levels. The only substantial light was available from Crown Court. (Author)

estranged from his wife, was increasingly suffering from the affects of alcoholism which would ultimately lead to his resignation as surveyor to the Grosvenor Estate in 1910 and his death in 1911.

The 'Kirk of the Crown of Scotland' had occupied its site at Crown Court since 1719 but between 1832 and 1879 it reached the high point in its history under the ministry of the Revd Dr John Cumming. It was then decided to establish a new church called St Columba's in Kensington, which was closer to most of the congregation. As a result, it was expected that the old church would close. However, many members remained loyal, notably Lord Balfour of Burleigh, and it survived. Unfortunately, it had a much-reduced congregation, few of whom were wealthy, and the building began to fall into disrepair so that rainy Sundays required the use of umbrellas.[41] With continuing deterioration, there was concern that the church would be closed and pulled down. At this point help for the repair or rebuilding was enlisted from Lady Francis Balfour, wife of Eustace Balfour. It was largely due to her determination that funds were raised for rebuilding.

Balfour Turner were, not surprisingly, appointed as architects for the new church, intended to seat 480 and which would incorporate a school and a church hall. The site was restricted, bounded by buildings on three sides with the only substantial daylight coming from Crown Court. The main entrance was via a corridor and an external doorway situated in Russell Street. There was a limited budget for the new building and Turner's solution was to locate the school and hall at ground-floor level, then place the church on the floor above, as a double-height space, using galleries around three sides to double the seating capacity. He presented three proposals for the ground floor. The first included living quarters for the caretaker, the second proposed small rooms divided off from the main hall by a brick wall, and the third included screens to divide the classrooms from the main hall. Due to lack of funds, the church reluctantly decided to proceed with the third option.[42]

The structure was innovative, featuring the early use of steel framing, concealed by timber cladding, to maximise space and speed construction. Like other Arts and Crafts architects, Turner was very interested in the use of new materials and building techniques. For example, at Westbrook, he used mass concrete for the floor construction and steel trusses for the roof.

The main entrance from Russell Street is marked by stone pilasters and a pediment with the word 'Holy' in large stone lettering above the name of church set in a semi-circular arch. The main body of the building can only be seen from Crown Court and is built of red brickwork, enlivened by Portland stone dressings. It is in a Jacobean-inspired, Free Style design as often favoured by Balfour Turner.

The elevation rises from the pavement edge and the articulation of the façade is limited to maximise internal space. Lady Balfour described the simplicity of surface treatment as 'dignity and restrained grace.'[43] Towers are placed at each end of the elevation, projecting slightly forward of the main wall plane. At ground level these towers contain secondary entrances into the building. The southerly one is surmounted by an open, pedimented stone pavilion, whilst the northerly tower features a crenellated parapet. The two towers are linked by a parapet of

stone and diagonally latticed terracotta. To maximise lighting in the building, the elevation is extensively glazed with mullion and transomed windows. Additional light comes from a clerestory set behind the parapet. The windows to the ground-floor school and hall extend down to the pavement level and are protected by finely crafted wrought-iron railings.

The Jacobean theme of the exterior is continued in the interior decoration. Dark coloured oak timberwork adds warmth while the use of slender, timber clad, steel columns enhance the lightness of the church. The main floor of the church is able to seat 275, whilst another 213 people can be seated in the galleries.

The main visual feature is a colourful Hanoverian coat-of-arms (reflecting the foundation of the old church in 1718) above the communion table. Below the arms is a St Andrew's cross intertwined with Scottish thistles and English roses. This was carved by Laurence Turner who was also responsible for the decoration to the organ case, the communion table, the baptismal font and Burning Bush emblem at the entrance.

Like St Anselm's, the Crown Court Church is a work of great originality, demonstrating Turner's dislike of the Gothic Revival and his refusal to conform to mainstream church design. It would appear from the church accounts that the partners did not charge fee for their work.[44] It continues to be used by the Church of Scotland and is an outstanding example of a church built on a restricted urban site for a limited budget, using innovative new construction techniques and materials.

Later years

The death of Eustace Balfour on the 14 February 1911 had a major affect on Turner and was followed by the death on the 11 May 1911, of John Kent, the assistant secretary of the SPAB. As a result Turner, aged 59 resigned as secretary of the SPAB, the 1912 SPAB *Report* stating: 'The Society has received a serious blow in the resignation of its Secretary, Mr. Thackeray Turner, after twenty-nine years of indefatigable activity for the protection of

Fig. 13: The interior of Crown Court Church in 1944. The slender timber columns conceal the structural steel framework. The coat of arms was carved by Laurence Turner. (English Heritage/NMR)

Ancient Buildings. It is impossible to overstate the debt, which the Society, and those who share its principles, owes to Mr. Turner's service.'[45]

As his replacement Turner recommended the architect A. R. Powys, who had trained in SPAB techniques with William Weir, and was to be a key figure in the continued success of the SPAB between the wars. Within six months Turner had taken Powys into partnership in Balfour Turner. Turner retired in 1923, and in 1925 Powys took John Macgregor OBE, into partnership, changing the name of the practice to Powys Macgregor.[46] Turner continued to be involved with the SPAB, undertaking building inspections and also serving as chairman of the SPAB Committee until his death in 1937.

Conclusion

Thackeray Turner trained and worked for two of the nineteenth-century's most important church architects. However, he came to despise the work of the Gothic Revival and he felt a deep horror of the effect it had on the destruction of medieval churches. He fully embraced the conservation principles of William Morris and Philip Webb and, through his work with the SPAB, ensured these principles were continued into the twentieth century.

In conjunction with Eustace Balfour, he only designed two churches but both these exhibit great originality in planning and design. They were conceived to purposely rebel against contemporary church design of the period. These churches show his love of historic buildings, but also his reverence in the way he chose not to mimic their appearance. Turner's honesty in design matched the integrity of his character.

Notes

1   Ian Nairn & Nikolaus Pevsner, *The Buildings of England, Surrey* (Harmondsworth, 1971), 259.

2   Ibid., 292.

3   F. H. W. Sheppard (ed.) *Survey of London: Volume 39* (London, 1977).

4   F. W. Troup, 'Thackeray Turner', Journal of the Royal Institute of British Architects, 45 (1938), 258.

5   Gavin Stamp, *An Architect of Promise: George Gilbert Scott Junior (1839–1897) and the Late Gothic Revival* (Donnington, 2002), 21.

6   Troup, 'Thackeray Turner', 258.

7   H. Thackeray Turner, Account Book, 6 April 1878, SPAB Archive.

8   Geoffrey K. Brandwood, *Temple Moore: An Architect of the Late Gothic Revival* (Stamford, 1997) does not mention Thackeray Turner, although the two men would have known each other. Their careers took very different paths.

9   Stamp, *An Architect of Promise*, 350. Apart from Thackeray Turner's involvement at Knapton church, Stamp does not specifically link him to any other projects although as Scott's chief assistant he would have been involved in many of them.

10 Ibid., 209–54, contains a detailed account of his attitude to conservation and involvement with the SPAB.

11 Ibid., 225–6, describes Scott's work and the involvement of the SPAB and Balfour.

12 Ibid., 231–5, describes Scott's and the SPAB's involvement in the restoration work.

13 Quoted in ibid., 234.

14 Ibid.

15 H. Thackeray Turner, Account Book, 13 December 1882, SPAB Archive.

16 Stamp, *An Architect of Promise*, 319–42, describes Scott's decline in detail.

17 Chris Miele (ed.), *From William Morris Building Conservation and the Arts and Crafts Cult of Authenticity*, 1877–1939 (New Haven & London, 2005), 51–2.

18 H. Thackeray Turner, *SPAB Annual Review* 1927, SPAB Archive, 13–16.

19 H. Thackeray Turner, *SPAB Annual Review* 1886, SPAB Archive, 45–7.

20 H. Thackeray Turner, *SPAB Annual Review* 1896, SPAB Archive, 7–14.

21 W. R. Lethaby, *Philip Webb and his Work* (Oxford, 1935).

22 H. Thackeray Turner, *SPAB Annual Review* 1896, SPAB Archive, 9.

23 Michael Drury, *Wandering Architect: In Pursuit of an Arts and Crafts Ideal* (Stamford, 2000), 32–6, 94–9, gives accounts of both projects.

24 Ibid., 25.

25 C. Powell & R. E. Wills, *A Family Memoir* (privately published, London, 1903).

26 Quintin Watt, *The Bromsgrove Guild* (Bromsgrove Society, 1999), 7.

27 A. Stuart Gray, *Edwardian Architecture* (London, 1985), 99–100. In 1879, Balfour married Lady Francis Cambell, later a prominent suffragette, daughter of the 8th duke of Argyll, and sister of the 9th duke of Argyll, who married Queen Victoria's daughter, the Princess Louise.

28 'Men Who Build, Number 49', *Builders' & Architectural Record*, 24 March 1897, 87.

29 Ibid., 88.

30 F. H. W. Sheppard (ed.) *Survey of London: Volume 39* (London, 1977).

31 Quoted in F. H. W. Sheppard (ed.) *Survey of London: Volume 40* (London, 1980), 77–9.

32 Troup, 'Thackeray Turner', 258.

33 Ibid., 77.

34 Ibid., 79.

35 Ibid.

36 Ibid., 77–79: 'Men Who Build, Number 49', *Builders' & Architectural Record*, 24 March 1897, 88–9.

37 Ibid., 89.

38 *Architectural Association Notes*, 10, 1896, 174.

39 Sheppard, *Survey of London: Volume 40*, 79.

40 Ibid., 79.

41 J. B. Huffman, 'For Kirk and Crown: The Rebuilding of the Crown Court Church, 1905–1909', *The London Journal*, 17 (1992), 56.

42 Ibid., 60.

43 Ibid., 62.

44 Ibid., 65.

45 *SPAB Report 1938*, SPAB Archive, 9.

46 S. J. Powys Marks, 'A. R. Powys: A Sketch of his Life and Work', *The Powys Review*, 10:3 (1982), 53.

Robin Stannard can be contacted at r.stannard@scottbrownrigg.com

Review Essay
by Gavin Stamp

John Salmon, *Ernest Charles Shearman (1859–1939) An Anglo-Catholic Architect: An Illustrated Introduction to his Life and Work.* The Anglo-Catholic History Society, London, 2009, 194 pp., 199 b&w pls, £20.00, pbk, ISBN: 978 0 9560565 0 4.

The work of E. C. Shearman is puzzling. Three years younger than Temple Moore, he designed his first significant church – in Wimbledon – in Edward VII's reign when he was in his late forties. This remarkably original, idiosyncratic building was followed by five other London churches, all very similar in style and configuration, over the following two decades. All have the same Gerona Cathedral plan with narrow passage aisles and a wide nave covered by a roof on arched timber beams springing from below the generous clerestory; all have a narrower aisled chancel, terminating in a semi-circular apse; all have the same distinctive mannerisms and very peculiar flush transepts; all were faced externally with a purplish brick while internal surfaces are of hard, utilitarian Flettons combined with render. What seems particularly extraordinary is that no stylistic development is evident in this series of churches, and that the same materials as well as plan were used despite changes in taste and more difficult economic conditions after the intervening Great War.

John Salmon has performed a most useful service by assembling all the information that we have about Shearman, reproducing some of his surviving letters and sketches and giving a detailed history of his churches, with illustrations. This, however, is the sort of history that deals with the minutiae of liturgical arrangements and concentrates on such facts as which bishop laid the foundation stone and listings of the names of all the incumbents in each church. Questions which the highly distinctive, not to say peculiar design of those churches inevitably beg are not asked, let alone answered. Despite all the research, E. C. Shearman remains as much of a mystery as ever. (His grandson, Professor John Shearman, would seem to have known little about his forebear, at least to judge by an uninformative essay on his work by Christopher D. H. Row in a *festschrift* to the late art historian published in 2001.)

Ernest Charles Shearman was born in Sheffield in 1859. In 1876 he was articled to and subsequently worked as an assistant for Charles Barry junior, whose rather pedestrian Gothic Revival churches would seem to have had little or no influence on Shearman's own architecture. He also attended the Royal

Academy Schools and 'travelled a little' in France and Italy. All very conventional. Then, in 1888, Shearman crossed the Atlantic to work in Argentina for three years. By his own account, he was 'Architect to the Buenos Aires Great Southern Railway'. Founded in 1862, the Ferrocarril Gran Sud de Buenos Aires was the largest of the several British-owned railways in Argentina, but in a recent detailed study of the railway architecture in that country (Jorge D. Tartarini, *Arquitectura Ferroviara*, Buenos Aires 2005), there is no mention whatsoever of Shearman: presumably he merely acted as an assistant to other architects. Returning to England at the end of 1891, he settled in Winchester where he designed a house for his mother (in which he later lived himself). He then worked under Robert W. Edis as resident architect at Sandringham and for the rebuilding of Cheveley Park near Newmarket. After setting up in practice on his own, Shearman was responsible for a building for an epileptic home at Chalfont St Peter and for the design of a few rectories.

Then, in about 1906, Shearman suddenly and inexplicably emerged as a mature and sophisticated architect, for nothing in his *curriculum vitae* prepares one for the very unusual, highly mannered design of St Matthew's Wimbledon; a brick church Shearman had designed earlier in Zamora, a suburb of Buenos Aires, seems to be a very pedestrian and uninteresting affair, exhibiting not a hint of what was to come. The Wimbledon church, on which work began in 1908, no longer stands as it was largely demolished by a V1 in 1944, but it set the pattern for what followed. Next came the best known and most accessible of Shearman's churches, that of St Silas the Martyr, Kentish Town (1911–13), closely followed by St Barnabas', Pitshanger Lane, in the new garden suburb of Brentham in North Ealing (1913–17). After the war came St Gabriel's, Acton (1929–32, incomplete), St Barnabas', Temple Fortune (1931–62), and, finally, the church of St Francis of Assisi at Isleworth, on the Great West Road (1933–5).

Why the founders of these churches were all prepared to build near repeats of St Matthew's, Wimbledon, is not known, but evidently Shearman had good connections in the Anglo-Catholic world in London. This patronage is remarkable, nevertheless, as Shearman's style was clearly unfashionable in its time. These grand churches received very few mentions in the architectural press and none of them was illustrated either in Nicholson's & Spooner's *Recent Ecclesiastical Architecture* (1911) or in the books later published by the Incorporated Church Building Society, *New Churches Illustrated* (1936) and *Fifty Modern Churches* (1947). What did he think he was doing? Shearman himself wrote of St Silas' that, 'The Church is designed on the Basilican model with wide nave affording the whole congregation an uninterrupted view of the Sanctuary and Pulpit; the Altar being the centre of the Apse', but he did not explain his style or his sources. Bridget Cherry has written of Shearman's 'passionate Mediterranean Gothic' and S. Antonio in Padua and Sta Croce in Florence have been suggested as sources of inspiration, but such buildings are not what immediately come to mind when contemplating Shearman's idiosyncratic style.

Shearman's churches are certainly Gothic. Most have Flowing Decorated tracery in the tall thin windows and several have large rose windows with elaborate Flowing tracery patterns of great beauty. Other details are very angular, however, and his buttresses are thin and flat. Amongst Shearman's several repetitious mannerisms are his transepts, flush with the aisles, which are terminated by a low pitched gable, above which is a recessed triangular gable rising above the eaves in line with the clerestory. These features have little expression internally. Another strange personal mannerism is the presence of square towers, occasionally terminating in a turret, placed between the eastern transepts and the apse. Apart from containing chimney flues, these thin towers have no real function, and it is surely extraordinary to find an architect repeating such expensive mannerisms over and over again.

At first, Shearman's highly original interpretation of Gothic would seem to have no English precedents. With their angular details and extensive use of brickwork – especially the internal hard industrial brick – his churches might seem to have more in common with Continental experiments in the early twentieth century, with Dutch Expressionism, for instance. Interestingly, back in 1952 Nikolaus Pevsner described the interior of St Silas' as 'Remarkably original, if somewhat mannered', helpfully adding that there is 'perhaps a little of the character or Berlage's work'. The brick churches of Dom Paul Bellot might also come to mind. However, there are in fact English parallels. C. H. B. Quennell's church in Upper Edmonton, dating from 1905–6, is similar in its buttressed angularity and in the use of simple, expressive brick forms internally, while the combination of simplified arches with plain plastered surfaces had appeared earlier in the work of Temple Moore (whose canted west end at St Wilfrid's Harrogate may explain the similar shape of the west end of St Silas'). Giles Scott's tracery patterns may well have influenced Shearman's while his first design for Liverpool Cathedral might possibly lie behind his very peculiar transept design, though the motif of a slightly recessed gable above a straight parapet appeared earlier in the church designs of Leonard Stokes (who was one of Shearman's three proposers when he became an Associate of the RIBA in 1892). In the absence of evidence, however, all this must be speculation – and those distinctive transepts are essentially a most original design.

What Shearman seems to have done in Wimbledon was to integrate ideas from the latest English church architecture with the High Victorian aesthetic – with the 'bare style' of the brick slum churches by Brooks, and G .E. Street's ideas about the proper characteristics of a Town Church. The dominant, unbroken roofline of Shearman's churches recalls that of St Augustine's Pendlebury by Bodley & Garner. In his book, John Salmon inadvertently offers a clue by quoting a letter of 1908 in which Shearman wrote that, 'The late Mr Pearson taught me not to put the font away in a corner', for that architect's work may well explain much of Shearman's. Eastern towers framing an apsed chancel – a feature which occurs in German Romanesque work – were used by Pearson at St Michael's Croydon, while the Gerona Cathedral plan (if with a square-ended chancel) was employed at St John's, Red Lion Square, for instance. Precedents alone, however, cannot explain the sudden originality of Shearman's work – nor why he felt obliged to repeat himself over and over again. There are other examples of that, of course; Soane had developed the essence of his own personal style by the 1790s and Summerson suggested he had no new ideas after that but repeated and developed his stock of motifs. But Soane was young when he developed his style; Shearman was almost fifty when he emerged as a highly idiosyncratic designer. One debunking explanation might be that, for the Wimbledon job, Shearman employed a gifted assistant, and then repeated the formula again and again as he could do nothing else. But if that was the case, it surely could not have been kept a secret – certainly not from H. S. Goodhart-Rendel who was privy to most Edwardian architectural gossip.

Goodhart-Rendel did not like St Silas', Kentish Town. In a paragraph taken (without acknowledgement) from Basil Clarke's *Parish Churches of London*, John Salmon quotes him as finding a 'sinister artiness' about the church, and that 'everything seems to be deliberately unmeaning and odd'. I can go further. Some thirty years ago, I took an interest in Shearman's churches and wrote to the late Sir John Summerson to ask about a visit I gathered he had paid to St Silas' with Goodhart-Rendel (this must have been in the later 1940s, by which time Rendel had become a Roman Catholic and was doubtless irritated by extreme Anglo-Catholicism). Summerson replied (12th February 1978) that

He *hated* it. "over-sexed" he said and went on to say something faintly scandalous about Shearman and vicars' wives. It *may* of course have been what I believe is called an "extrapolation" from the (to him) obviously adulterous character of the architecture [although Mr Salmon, on page 28 of his book, suggests a more literal interpretation might have been intended]. When I said I liked the church he got quite cross and involuntarily dipped his hand into the holy-water stoup. Realising that the water was anglican he gave the hand a brisk shake. [...] Shearman is terribly mannered but I do rather like St Silas. I wish I knew more of his work.

I, too, rather like St Silas's, although the pointless extravagance of the inaccessible and useless spaces within the non-transepts, along with Shearman's other mannerisms, can also be exasperating. And to find the same tricks being played, two decades on, in dreary outer London suburbs is rather sad as well as perplexing. Much as I long to know more about his curious career, perhaps it is for the best that Shearman remains an enigma.

Book reviews

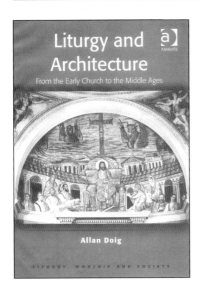

Allan Doig, *Liturgy and Architecture From the Early Church to the Middle Ages*. Ashgate, Aldershot, 2008, xxii + 224 pp., 10 col. plates, 48 b&w plates, £15.99 pbk, ISBN 978 0 7545 5274 8.

Liturgy and Architecture examines the evolution of the forms of eastern and western churches in the context of the development of liturgy from the earliest buildings used for Christian worship to the thirteenth century. Chronologically arranged chapters help to make the broad development easy to follow. Supporting illustrations are adequate rather than lavish; they would have been enhanced by the inclusion of a few more plans and some specially produced drawings showing the pattern of ceremonial movement.

Within each chapter discussion proceeds by way of example. In most instances there is a concentration on one or two churches either because they are of particular historical significance, and/or because they are particularly well researched and understood, and/or because written sources exist which help to elucidate the ways in which they were used. These major examples are often supplemented, particularly in the late antique period, by shorter discussion of others to illuminate particular points. The rare juxtaposition of architectural evidence and evidence of ceremonial (reconstructed from both liturgical texts and contemporary historical accounts) leads to some illuminating and striking description, particularly, for example, of the sixth-century Hagia Sophia (pp. 68–78), while the chronological and geographical range of the book, which includes the Byzantine as well and the Western tradition, facilitates comparison between both periods and places in a way rarely achieved.

Within this impressive framework, there is an inevitable concentration on greater churches, since it is for them that surviving liturgical texts were written, or for great political events held within them that there are surviving textual accounts. The politics of patronage and of imperial and royal occasions is fully discussed, but lightly, supporting rather than over-loading the main architectural and liturgical momentum of the text.

There is some unevenness of coverage, most strikingly in the final section on Gothic architecture. It is not quite clear whether Christopher Wilson's statement that Gothic architecture and contemporary liturgy 'showed remarkably little interaction' is quoted (p. 170) with approval or questioningly, but to discuss the whole period from the mid-twelfth to the end of the sixteenth in under thirty pages and by way of only four examples, one in France (S. Denis) and three in England (late twelfth-century Canterbury and Wells; early thirteenth-century Salisbury), spoils the balance achieved in the earlier sections of the book.

Readers with a primary interest in early church and in the period (in the west) up to the rise of the Use of Sarum in the thirteenth century will find here a useful and readable overview of complicated and diverse material. Despite its short length and convenient format, it is far from superficial, and it provides an entry into a subject which has for too long been the preserve of a few specialists. The paperback is, moreover, most reasonably priced.

P. S. Barnwell, Kellogg College, University of Oxford

Nigel Yates, *Liturgical Space Christian Worship and Church Buildings in Western Europe 1500–2000*. Ashgate, 2008, xi +199 pp., 35 b&w plates, 36 line drawings, £17.99 pbk ISBN 978 0 7546 5797 2.

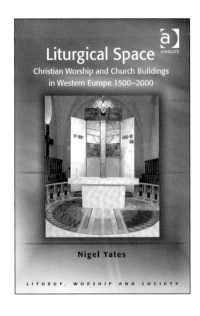

This is an amazing book that is tight on focus and breathtaking in its geographical reach through north-western Europe and Scandinavia, and over such a vast period of time. It is fitting tribute to Nigel Yates, who sadly died last year, that he is perhaps the only author one can imagine undertaking this venture. He provides a clear outline of the legacy of the early church and the impact of the Reformation on Christian architecture, explores its variations in Lutheran and Calvinist settings in Europe, reveals what happened in England – thus setting Archbishop Laud's work in context – comments on what happened in Counter-Reformation Catholic countries, and really comes into his own when explaining the origins and extent of the Gothic revival, its ethos, and the impact of liturgical renewal upon church designs in the twentieth century. It is an amazing *tour de force*. The work is magisterial in tone, peppered with wonderful examples, lavishly illustrated with photographs, diagrams and architectural plans. There is a useful guide to further reading and an even more useful guide to buildings to visit in fourteen countries. The book is clearly a product of his life's work and years of visiting churches across the continent, and it complements rather than supplants earlier books for which Yates is justly famous. Possibly because it is overflowing with details and packs so much in about both liturgy and architecture, it is not the easiest of books to read. It gets better when dealing with his trademark explosion of myths about the Gothic revival. Yates is excellent in revealing complexities and regional variations in his story; he is a learned guide. In one sense he is perhaps too authoritative, for this reader would have appreciated more comment on how we know all this, who were some of the key people behind these changes, and how much depended on particular bishops in certain dioceses and what we might learn about regional traditions in church architecture. Nevertheless, it is a tribute to the ambitious, broad sweep of this book – the way in which it culls material from both Protestant and Catholic camps, and from across northern Europe – that Nigel Yates has provided a rich, satisfying work that provokes questions to the very end.

Andrew Foster, Universities of Southampton and Kent

David Stancliffe, *The Lion Companion to Church Architecture*. Lion Hudson, Oxford, 2008, 288 pp., around 550 col. plates, £20.00 hdbk, ISBN 978 0 7459 5190 4.

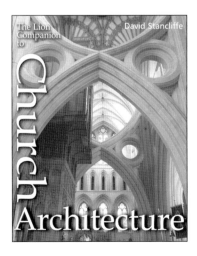

This is a splendid book and should be compulsory reading for all architectural historians, not because they will learn anything further about architectural history, but because it will show them a very different way of looking at religious buildings.

First it is a lavish publication by Lion Hudson of Oxford. Colour is used throughout on good quality glossy art paper and the sewn sections are bound within a hard cover and jacket, both of which have a spectacular image of the inside of Wells Cathedral printed on them – this is a nice touch. The only negatives are that there are a few widows and orphans and some may dislike the occasional overlaying of images and text.

The chapters follow a chronological pattern – the Renaissance follows the Gothic Vision, and in turn is followed by the Reformation and the Gothic Revival before finally Chapter 10 goes in search of a "Genuine, 'Modern' Church Architecture".

There is an index of terms and another of churches, and a list of suggested titles for further reading, though this is somewhat limited in scope. There is also a useful glossary. The text is not footnoted; much to the delight of some and the regret of others.

The great strength of this book is that it moves ecclesiastical architecture away from the purely structural into a much wider arena. For instance the chapter on the Gothic Revival mentions Goethe, Schiller, Beethoven and Schubert in the 4th line and Wordsworth, Keats, Blake and Turner in the 7th. The architectural changes that flowed are put firmly within a wider context of continuity and of change. A reasonably rapid canter through the changes that dominated much of the nineteenth century follows, and while this may not be of great interest to the specialist, it does provide a good overview for the less knowledgeable.

I particularly enjoyed the chapters that are more conceptual in their approach. What is a spiritual space? Is it just a piece of architectural construction? Well, if you read chapter 1 you will see that it clearly is not. Likewise chapter 10 explores the development of church design in the twentieth century and the emphasis on the building as 'a house of the people of God' rather than 'a house for God', a place for communal worship rather than a place for private devotion. Rather astutely Stancliffe cites some words uttered by the architect Frederick Gibberd who designed the Roman Catholic Cathedral of Christ the King in Liverpool: 'Church architecture is indifferent because the Church is ignorant of architecture: it does not know how to choose an architect and, having chosen one, it does not understand how to brief him' (p. 254). Perhaps this book should be compulsory reading for all clergy.

What emerges is that perhaps we need to be occasionally reminded that churches were not primarily built as architectural wonders but as spaces that would declare the glory of God and provide space for his worship. They took the form and style that was both fashionable at the time they were built and which suited the liturgy that applied then. As times change so do fashions and liturgy is no different. Perhaps we should be more willing to accept change and less intent upon conservation.

John Elliott, formerly of the University of Reading

Lynne Broughton, *Interpreting Ely Cathedral*. Ely Cathedral Publications, 2008, 241 pp., 290 col. plates, £14.99 pbk, ISBN 978 1 873027 11 0.

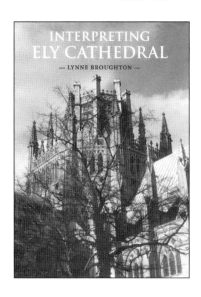

Lynne Broughton has written a Christian guide to Ely Cathedral for the twenty-first century. Her *Interpreting Ely Cathedral* is written for a general audience with an interest in the Christian faith and follows a route around the building that a modern visitor might take. While grounded in the medieval architecture, furnishings and decoration it nonetheless attends to the Victorian and more recent additions with equal regard. This is because Broughton's intention is to demonstrate how the cathedral functioned, and continues to function, as a symbol of heaven in the Christian faith. This basic parallel between all churches and the Heavenly Jerusalem is the principle upon which the diverse features of the building are here reintegrated. It is also used by the author as a device to explore the particular approach to this idea in the construction and furnishing of Ely Cathedral.

The present volume is intended as a complement to several major publications on Ely Cathedral. The author draws upon this rich body of literature to weave a holistic vision of the site. Careful referencing throughout directs the inquisitive reader to these and other sources. However, the author's own beliefs and religious profession form the emotional core of the work. On a few occasions, the author departs from the established literature to suggest alternative interpretations based upon the practice of the religion. In one particular instance, she rightly criticises the insufficient attention paid to the marginal details of church furnishings as compared to the marginal details of illuminated manuscripts. Whether or not it is possible to confirm her alternative reading of the choir stalls through comparative visual analysis, it usefully highlights the need for a reconsideration of them.

Throughout the book, the author demonstrates the role of imagery in maintaining the continuity of the Christian faith. Fittingly the book is illustrated at every opportunity with colour photography, the principal delight of this accessible and engaging paperback. Indeed, underlying this publication is a deep sense of enjoyment and appreciation of the wonders and curiosities to be found in the detail of this magnificent edifice. It is a road map for how the building can continue to inspire and nurture the spiritual development of those pilgrims who continue to arrive at its door.

Rosie Mills, Victoria and Albert Museum

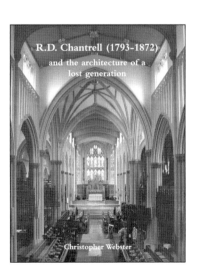

Christopher Webster, *R. D. Chantrell (1793–1872) and the architecture of a lost generation*. Spire Books, 2010, 347 pp., 193 b&w pls, £30.00 hdbk, ISBN 978 1 904965 22 0.

This is an important book, attractively produced to Spire Books' customary high standard, with an interesting range of contemporary illustrations and modern photographs.

The book's importance is threefold. Firstly: there is no doubting Chantrell's significance - a pupil of Soane, prolific, varied and occasionally innovative, he was responsible for one of the outstanding churches of the early nineteenth century (St Peter's, Leeds 1837–41) -

and Webster provides a valuable account of his life and a critical assessment of his works together with a comprehensive *catalogue raisonné*. Secondly: Chantrell's career straddles a period that saw the emergence of the modern architectural practice and profession. He was the first Leeds architect to be elected to the recently founded Institute of British Architects and became 'something of a pioneer in seeking to supply architectural services of the highest professional standards in the provinces' (p. 163). Chapter 6 analyses the workings of Chantrell's office, something of an achievement given the lack of a business archive, and is especially useful since there are so few published accounts of the nuts and bolts of architectural practice at this time. So, altogether, this is an invaluable reference work that should be on the shelves of all students of the period.

Thirdly, Webster offers a compelling thesis that should stimulate debate and research in this neglected area. The title of the book indicates his standpoint. That the genius of Pugin and the polemical prose of the *Ecclesiologist* (the latter dubbed by Chantrell as 'a mischievous tissue of imbecility and fanaticism') have distorted critical perceptions of the architecture, and especially the churches, of the first half of the nineteenth century is now widely recognised. A growing number of revisionist studies of the (particularly Anglican) church in the last decades of the 'long eighteenth century' should caution critics from making knee-jerk and dismissive assessments of the buildings of the period. But Webster takes us further: Chantrell's career underlines the scale of the achievement of the pre-Puginian generation of church builders, especially those working in the Gothic idiom. Trained rigorously in the Classical mode, Chantrell - an active antiquarian - moved beyond the observation of Gothic detail to capture the true principles and spirit of the style (his system of proportions was influential at the time). The shifting focus of authors such as John Britton and E. J. Wilson - Webster is strong on his analysis of contemporary architectural literature and its readers - indicates a growing recognition by architects in the 1820s, '30s and '40s of the need for models from which to help master Gothic. Wider issues are also raised. Architects were not responding simply to a top-down requirement for Gothic from an influential Church party or Church Commissioners bent on economy, but as much to grass roots demand, a 'mania', for plain Gothic on the part of parochial vestries. The extent of this popular attachment to the associational values of Gothic during the first thirty years of the nineteenth century deserves further study.

Martin Cherry

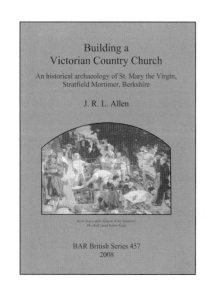

J. R. L. Allen, *Building a Victorian Country Church*. British Archaeological Reports, 457, 2008, xi + 140 pp., many b&w pls, £31.00 pbk, ISBN 978 1 4073 0262. J. R. L. Allen, *Late Churches and Chapels in Berkshire*. BAR 432, 2007, xi + 162 pp., many b&w pls, £36.00 pbk, ISBN 978 1 407300375. J. R. L. Allen, *Carrstone in Norfolk Buildings*. BAR 371, 2004, viii + 162 pp., many col. and b&w pls, £38.00 pbk, ISBN 1841716138.

For most aficionados of English churches, building materials play second fiddle to architectural style, patronage, internal decoration and liturgical arrangements. Yet much of the visual impact of any church depends on its materials, and nowhere more so than in the nineteenth century, when railways cut the cost of transport and architects strove for ever more bold and original effects. As a professional geologist, J. R. L. Allen is well-qualified to write on these matters, and his books betray his scientific background. They are published in the format of archaeological reports, with sober covers, the text arranged in double columns and the chapters divided into sections, each with a 'discussion' at the end summarising the material presented earlier. Each is copiously supplied with tables, and there are plenty of distribution maps, appendices and photographs, mostly in black and white. For Allen, churches primarily as artefacts, and religious life plays little part in his analyses. His prose is workmanlike rather than elegant. Yet his potentially Gradgrindish approach yields rewarding results.

Churches merit only one chapter in *Carrstone in Norfolk Buildings*, among them the medieval parish church at Sandringham, much remodelled by S. S. Teulon and Arthur Blomfield, and a scattering of Nonconformist chapels, all in the dark brown stone peculiar to the north and north-west of the county. But they assume centre stage in the two volumes on Berkshire. This is a county which lost its two largest ecclesiastical buildings – the abbeys at Abingdon and Reading – at the Dissolution. With a few exceptions, notably St George's Chapel in Windsor Castle, its remaining medieval churches are not particularly large or especially architecturally distinguished. But prosperity came in the nineteenth century, and it brought with it a vigorous programme of church-building and restoration, both in the expanding towns and in the villages and hamlets in which most of the population still lived. It is this achievement which is idiosyncratically celebrated in *Late Churches and Chapels in Berkshire* (Berkshire meaning the historic, pre-1974 county).

Like most of south-east England, Berkshire is not very well supplied with building stone, and some of the county's Victorian churches are built of imported materials. So Henry Woodyer used a hard carboniferous sandstone from the Mendips at Christ Church, Reading (1862–74), one his best churches. At Fawley (1864–6), on the Downs, G. E. Street, another architect who designed some of his best churches in Berkshire, used small, rough blocks of Bath stone. More often, local materials were also pressed into service, some of them not at all obvious: Bargate rubble (more commonly found over the Surrey border) at Sandhurst (Street, 1853–4); sarsens at Sotwell, a small village church of 1884 by the very obscure S. R. Stephenson; and brown Corallian sandstone in Pugin's little church of 1844–7 at Tubney, built for an Anglican friend, J. R. Bloxham. As in the Middle Ages, the most commonly used local stone was flint, and it was sometimes handled in a highly inventive manner, as at Teulon's extraordinary church at Leckhampstead (1858–60), where the flint is interspersed with horizontal bands of brick. Brick was an even more common material, and was used with great polychromatic panache in Street's All Saints, Boyn Hill, Maidenhead (1854–7) – an archetypal High Victorian suburban church – and in Nonconformist chapels like the Baptist chapel at Wokingham, by the Reading firm of Poulton and Woodman. Allen has surprisingly little to say about brick-making, an important industry in Victorian Berkshire, and he largely ignores the use of internal use of polychromatic brick, as in Butterfield's beautifully preserved church at Beech Hill (1866–7). But his meticulous study nevertheless makes us look at Victorian churches in an unaccustomed light, while adding to our knowledge of the architectural riches of a somewhat neglected county.

Victorian churches have been much studied in recent years, but few have received the thorough treatment meted out by Allen to St Mary, Stratfield Mortimer. Here, as so often in Berkshire, we have a little-known church, built in 1866–9 with funds supplied by one of the county's largest landowners, Richard Benyon of Englefield House, just outside Reading. Little is known either about the architect, Richard Armstrong, who had already been employed by Benyon to enlarge Englefield House in a sumptuous neo-Jacobean style. His church at Stratfield Mortimer is a large and handsome essay, if somewhat conventional, essay in mid-Victorian 'Middle Pointed'. But it was always too large for the strictly functional needs of the village and is now rarely used, the focus of parish life having shifted to a smaller daughter church (also funded by Benyon, and designed by William Rhind. Armstrong's clerk of works) at the more populous settlement of Mortimer Common, a mile or so away.

The main interest of Allen's study (*Building a Victorian Country Church*) lies in its concentration on the process of building, a task made possible by the fortunate survival of a series of weekly returns by the clerk of works. The workforce, the supply of materials – mainly a limestone rubble from Swindon, brought by rail to the nearby Brunel-designed station – the organisation of the project, and the provision of furnishings and fittings: all are set out in an exhaustive fashion, and, as in the other books under review, there are useful appendices and a very full bibliography. The value of the book derives, paradoxically, from Stratfield Mortimer's very ordinariness. This was not an All Saints, Margaret Street, or a Holy Angels, Hoar Cross, built by famous architect for an aesthetically or ecclesiologically discerning patron; churches like Stratfield Mortimer can be found in almost every English county. But by chronicling the building history of one such church in such great detail Allen gives us a deeper insight into the rest, and for this he deserves the gratitude of anyone interested in the history of Victorian churches, and of Victorian England.

Geoffrey Tyack, Kellogg College, University of Oxford.

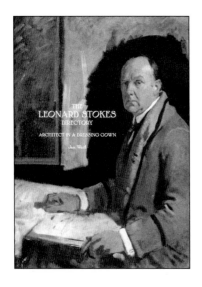

Jan Ward, *The Leonard Stokes Directory: Architect in a Dressing Gown*. Published by the author, 2009, 164 pp., many col. and b&w pls, £28.00 + £3.70 p&p pbk, ISBN 13 978 0 9534641 1 1. (Copies from www.leonardstokes.co.uk)

'A memorable building', wrote Pevsner of Leonard Stokes' church of St Clare, Sefton Park, Liverpool, praising its 'individuality' and its abandonment of the 'period precedent' seen in J. L. Pearson's nearby

Anglican church of St Agnes. Completed in 1890, St Clare's is unquestionably one of the key church buildings of the late Victorian period and as a pre-eminent Roman Catholic church architect (all of his churches were for the Roman Church) Lancashire-born Stokes (1858–1925) ranks alongside Pugin the elder, J. F. Bentley, G. G. Scott junior and Giles Scott. Had his proposed church in Miles Platting, Manchester, designed for the Norbertine Canons in 1892 but never constructed, been realised, Stokes' standing might be even higher – perspectives now in the RIBA collection confirm that this would have been a building of monumental power. Stokes' other built works included church schools and convents, the finest of the latter, at London Colney, Hertfordshire, for an Anglican sisterhood. (It is now a pastoral centre, owned by the Archdiocese of Westminster.) Not that Stokes' workload was entirely ecclesiastical: his secular projects included private houses, college buildings at Cambridge, an extension to J. M. Brydon's Chelsea Town Hall, and nineteen telephone exchanges.

For all the interest of Stokes' architecture, which often falls into the elusive category of 'Arts and Crafts Gothic', he remains a relatively obscure figure, with an article of 1946 in the *Architectural Review* and an *Oxford DNB* entry (by Peter Howell) the only significant published sources. The arrival of a book on Stokes' life and work is therefore to be warmly welcomed. Jan Ward's book is attractively produced and clearly reflects an interest in Stokes extending over many years. That said, Ward has produced neither a biography nor a critical account of the architecture. Entries in what appears to be a relatively complete catalogue of projects are based, however, almost entirely on secondary sources – Pevsner, list descriptions, journals and parish histories and websites – which are cited uncritically. Too much of the book has the appearance of a scrapbook and many of the photographs are of poor quality. Stokes' career was effectively cut short by the Parkinson's Disease which eventually killed him (though the onset of serious illness did not prevent him from assuming the RIBA Presidency in 1910). One longs to know more about the Stokes office, through which, at various times, Louis de Soissons, E. Vincent Harris, Albert Richardson, E. A. Rickards, William Weir and C. C. Winmill passed. In his own youth, Stokes had worked briefly for G. E. Street, one of the true founders of what became the Arts and Crafts movement. Stokes' relationship to the Arts and Crafts – his work was highly praised by C. R. Mackintosh – is one of the key issues on which this worthy, but in the end rather unsatisfactory, book barely touches.

Kenneth Powell

Stanley A. Shepherd, *The Stained Glass of A. W. N. Pugin*. Spire Books, 2009, 443 pp., 207 col. plates., £34.95 hdbk, ISBN 978 1 904965 20 6.

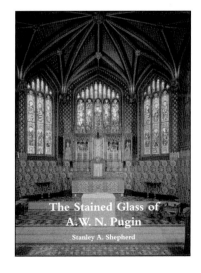

There is everything to praise and nothing to fault in this eagerly-awaited publication which is both an encyclopaedic work of reference and a book to delight all who have an interest in the life and work of Pugin and nineteenth-century stained glass generally. The extent of Pugin's achievements in this field is breathtaking; just how much was packed into a working life of little more than fifteen years, and yet stained glass was but one aspect of his revival of medieval art. For Pugin, however, as Stanley Shepherd points out, stained glass was 'the key on which the whole panoply of colour in the churches depended' (p.94).

Around half of Dr. Shepherd's 443-page book consists of a Gazetteer listing all of Pugin's known windows, both ecclesiastical and secular, in the context of their buildings. Arranged alphabetically in county order, each entry identifies the building, gives a detailed description of each window using the *Corpus Vitrearum* system of window referencing, then lists all the known documentation such as Pugin's letters (with extracts), company records (with prices charged), and published material relating to each window. Such comprehensive detail is not to be found in any other printed reference work. Do not, however, imagine that a book culled largely from a doctoral thesis (University of Birmingham, 1997) need necessarily be dull or over-technical. Dr. Shepherd has a lucid and engaging style, and the complex processes of glass design and production, and the development of styles, are all clearly explained. The text is enhanced by over a hundred superbly-produced colour plates, specially commissioned by Dr. Shepherd from photographer Alastair Carew-Cox. Entire windows, many occupying a whole page, are accompanied by close details, all crisply executed, giving a virtual tour of Pugin's work,

The Gazetteer is prefaced by an Introduction, and nine chapters on the various aspects of Pugin's work in stained glass. Particularly revealing is the account (Chapter 2) of Pugin's experiments in the actual production of coloured glass in his efforts to match the medieval samples he was able to acquire. In John Hardman Jnr. (1811–1867) – with whom Pugin was already working in the production of medieval-style metalwork – he had a friend and colleague who fully shared his ideas and also the Catholic Faith which was the driving force in all that he did. More importantly, it brought the whole process of glassmaking, from initial design to the finished product, under Pugin's control, although there were clear disadvantages in having the cartoon room at his family home in Ramsgate, and the actual production of the glass in Birmingham. Over a thousand letters passed between Pugin and Hardman, and Dr. Shepherd draws on these, and also on the extensive business records of the company, to give a very full account of their working arrangements

To have researched and written a Ph.D. thesis on so vast a subject in retirement, as Dr. Shepherd did, is admirable enough. That he proceeded to devote more years to the exacting task of adapting and presenting his work for publication in such an accessible and immensely attractive form deserves more than gratitude. The biggest surprise of all is the price: only £34.95. An invaluable tool for the researcher, it is also a book to be savoured, treasured, and enjoyed.

Michael Fisher

Other publications received

Roy Albutt, *A. E. Lemmon (1889–1963), Artist and Craftsman*. Roy Albutt, Pershore, 2008, 97 pp., 27 col. plates, £12.95 pbk, ISBN 978 0 9543566 2 0. (Copies can be obtained from 01386 552127).

Lemmon was born in Ladywood and trained at Birmingham School of Art. From c.1911 he worked in the stained glass studio of A. J. Davie of the Bromsgrove Guild. In 1927, Lemmon established his own studio in Bromsgrove from where he produced stained glass, painted altarpieces, processional crosses and other church fittings. He also taught at the Bromsgrove School of Art for over 20 years.

The book discusses Lemmon's life and work – and that of his son Peter – as well as cataloguing the firm's work.

Joyce A. Stephenson, *The Wood Carvings by William Gibbs Rogers for St Michael's Church, Cornhill*. Published by the author, 2009, 115pp, numerous colour plates, £39.00 hdbk (postage extra), ISBN 978 0 9812354 0 0. (Copies can be obtained from the author at jstephenson2@cogeco.ca)

Rogers was born in 1792, and in 1807 was apprenticed to a London carver. Evidently gifted, he set up in business in about 1816, and within a year was working at Carlton House, and later in the Throne Room at the Royal Pavilion as part of John Nash's refurbishment. In 1831 he decorated a suite of rooms in the new wing of Kensington Palace, and in 1850 was honoured with the commission by Queen Victoria of a cradle, now in the Kensington Palace Museum. As well as working as a woodcarver, with his own showroom, Rogers appears to have been a dealer in wood carvings, in 1834 mounting an exhibition of several hundred figures in boxwood and oak by fourteenth- and fifteenth-century carvers.

This exhibition also included work by Grinling Gibbons, for whom Rogers had a life-long admiration, stimulated by one of the elderly workmen he knew as an apprentice, who recalled working with carvers who had worked at St Paul's Cathedral under the direction of the great woodcarver. In about 1856 Rogers became engaged in restoring the work of Gibbons, adopting an approach – for example, at Belton House, Lincolnshire – which involved photographing the items before dismantling them and then using chemical methods to strengthen, preserve and recolour the original wood, reassembling the object from the photograph. Late in life he became increasingly passionate about restoring and preserving Gibbon's work, lecturing in 1875 on the topic to the RIBA.

Rogers' major church work includes the organ gallery front, pulpit and lectern at St Mary-at-Hill, City of London (1849; only the organ front survives, restored after the 1988 fire), a pulpit at St Anne's, Limehouse (1850s), and his carvings on the new pews, pulpit and lectern at St Michael's, Cornhill, City of London (begun 1858). The latter are the subject of this book, and occupy nearly one hundred of its pages, with detailed photographs of each of the large number of carved poppy-heads, the pulpit and the eagle lectern. Many of the bench-ends feature plants, and their symbolism is described. Some include texts: 'eminently Protestant', as *The Art Journal* said.

Trevor Jones, *Father Wilson of Haggerston, a life simply offered*. The Anglo-Catholic History Society, 2008, 64 pp., 21 b&w plates, £12.00 pbk, ISBN 978 0 95507 14 4 7. (Copies can be obtained from gbsbooks@connectfree.co.uk)

This is a memoir of Herbert Wilson (1890–1954) an Anglican priest who spent almost his entire career in Haggerston, Tower Hamlets, East London. The product of a devout middle class home and an Anglican public school, he exemplified the dutiful and reticent characteristics of a conservative Anglo-Catholic priest of that era, always addressing his colleagues by surname and following an austere way of life. He never married.

Despite his dedication to work, he found time to publish over 20 books about the active community life of his poor parish. Collectively these form a record of social life in a working class district of the East End during the 1920s and '30s. He remained in Haggerston throughout the Second World War and during the heaviest blitzes he could be seen about the parish in tin hat and cassock. He left behind a first hand account of living through bombing raids

After the war, he was faced with many changes including de-population but he did not live to see the closure of the church of St Augustine. Today it still stands but no longer in ecclesiastical use, a reminder of a vanished world.

John Martin Robinson, *Biddleston Chapel, Northumberland, a history and guide*. The Historic Chapels Trust, 2009, 36 pp., 29 plates, £10 inc. postage, pbk.
Biddleston chapel stands romantically perched above the ravine of the Biddle burn in the Upper Coquetdale valley – a remote moorland setting. The chapel is now an isolated structure, but until fifty years ago it was attached to a large Georgian country house, the former seat of the Selby family, who had owned the property since the reign of Edward II. The chapel itself was nineteenth-century but it was built within the thick stone shell of a fourteenth-century pele tower. It represented a continuous Catholic tradition from the Middle Ages. The lavishly illustrated booklet tells the story of the Selby family, the hall and its chapel, and of the Catholicism that survived in this isolated setting. It also contains a detailed description of the chapel, its monuments and a list of its known priests. It is an exemplary guide to a little known building, now diligently preserved by the Historic Chapels Trust.

... and a correction
We apologise for an error in the Reviews section of Issue 41. The book by Jane Allen, mentioned under 'other publications received' is correctly titled *The Wallace Connection* not *The Wallace Collection*.

The Ecclesiological Society

The Ecclesiological Society is for all those who love churches, and are interested in their fabric, furnishings and use. The Society was founded in 1879, as a successor to the Cambridge Camden Society of 1839. It has a lively programme, including various lectures, an annual conference, and visits to churches at a range of locations in the UK. Members receive the Society's periodical, *Ecclesiology Today*, twice a year.

Membership is open to all. For further details, see the Society's website at www.ecclsoc.org, or write to the Hon. Membership Secretary at the address given overleaf.

Contributions to *Ecclesiology Today*

The Editor is always pleased to receive articles for consideration for publication in *Ecclesiology Today*, or suggestions for proposed contributions, whether fully worked out or at an early stage in development. The Society wishes to encourage less-experienced authors, and the Editor is happy to provide informal support and guidance to those in this position.

In furtherance of the Society's aims, articles should promote 'the study of the arts, architecture and liturgy of the Christian Church'. They may be historical in nature, or reflect contemporary matters. They need not be restricted in time, place or denomination, and although in practice a significant number deal with Church of England churches, in recent years a wider range of material has been covered, a trend which it is wished to encourage. Articles dealing with individual buildings are welcome, although the Editor will expect the discussion to highlight matters of wider significance. The Society's interests cover a very wide field, and it is therefore important that articles should be written in a way which can be understood by anyone with a general interest in churches.

Most articles are objective and factual, but there is the opportunity for well-argued personal views on matters of general interest to be put forward in the occasional 'Viewpoint' series.

Prospective authors are invited to communicate with the Editor at the earliest possible stage. There is no formal process of refereeing, but articles will often be sent to one or more readers for an independent opinion before acceptance for publication, and eventual publication may be dependent upon the author making such modifications as the Editor, in consultation with the readers, may recommend.

Proposed contributions should preferably be submitted by email. They should be prepared in accordance with the style guide, available on the Society's website or by application to the Editor. Authors are reminded that they are responsible for any fees and permissions required for the reproduction of illustrations.

Books for review should be sent to the Reviews Editor. Material for *Church Crawler* should be sent to the News Editor.

The Ecclesiological Society